P9-DGJ-327

WEANING
AND HUMAN
DEVELOPMENT

Theodore Lownik Library
Illinois Benedictine College
Lisle, Illinois 60532

WEANING

AND HUMAN

DEVELOPMENT

GORDON R. FORRER, M. D.

Theodore Lownik Library
Illinois Benedictine College
Lisle, Illinois 60532

LIBRA PUBLISHERS, INC.

ROSLYN HEIGHTS, N.Y. 11577

155
.422
F 728w

FIRST EDITION

*All rights reserved, including the right of
reproduction in whole or in part in any form*

Copyright © 1969, by Libra Publishers, Inc.

391 Willets Road
Roslyn Heights, N.Y. 11577

Manufactured in the United States of America
Library of Congress Catalog Card Number: 72-79731

WEANING
AND HUMAN
DEVELOPMENT

"Medicine is not merely a science but an art. It does not consist in compounding pills and plasters and drugs of all kinds but it deals with the processes of life which must be understood before they can be guided."

Paracelsus

PREFACE

"Behold thou desirest truth in the inward parts:
and in the hidden part thou shalt make me to
know wisdom."

Psalms 51.6

Throughout recorded history, man has avoided truth.
Yet, he has also sought the truth. On the one hand, he has
shut his eyes, closed his ears, and cut himself off from
the obvious facts of his origin and his destiny. On the
other, there have been extraordinary people who have
marked the record by their persistent unwillingness to
accept false premises and unwarranted assumptions. Unfortunately, these people have represented a tiny fragment
of the human story.

Weaning and Human Development is a distinct contribution to the truth-seeking establishment. This book
challenges accepted concepts, embellishes them, and
forges ahead to create new and exciting ideas about the
origins of human behavior. It will be the reader's task to
decide for himself where this contribution will lie, both
in proportion to and in relative importance to the pioneering works in psychiatry.

Perhaps *Weaning and Human Development* will only
generate a ripple instead of a wave in the sea of psychiatric thought, but that ripple will be noticed by each
and every serious student of human behavior. It may not
generate a wave because it is far too challenging to fixed
ideas now being taught in our medical schools and in our
residency training centers. It may not generate a wave
because it is new—and anything new is accepted tenta-
tively, if at all, by most scientists. This is healthy and

as it should be. However, the immensity of this contribution will only be recognized after the research which it stimulates is completed.

The author of this book is not unknown to American psychiatry. He is already familiar as the developer of atropine coma therapy in the early 1950's. More recently, he has written "The Psychoanalytic Theory of Hallucinations" and "Psychoanalytic Theory of Placebo." I strongly recommend these papers to refresh the reader and stimulate his thinking in areas parallel to the present volume. He has also written an article on "Placebo," published in the Encyclopedia Britannica. He was formerly Assistant Professor of Psychiatry at Wayne State University Medical School, and is presently Chief of the Department of Psychiatry at Mt. Carmel Mercy Hospital, Detroit, Michigan.

I have had the privilege of knowing Dr. Forrer for a great many years. For approximately ten of those years the author and I have enjoyed lunch together on a monthly basis. At these luncheons we have discussed every topic imaginable related to our work. I was fortunate to have been present at the time the author was impregnated with the idea for this book. I have followed the arduous prenatal course. I was present during the labor pains, and I witnessed the delivery of the finished product.

As in any neonate, this book presents unanswered questions. It has always appeared to me that any new theory in psychiatry, any attempt to reexplain the old in terms of the new, conceives more questions than answers. This, in fact, may be the test of the greatness of anyone's contribution. New questions are then followed by more research and new answers, which in turn establish new questions. This is the endless path which science must pursue. This path must lead to a practical application of scientific knowledge to help the ego exert its mastery over the id and employ its energies in a totally constructive manner. A blanket of hope can then envelop mankind.

Weaning and Human Development is characterized by an intense intuitiveness and a searching perspicacity which can only evoke the admiration and interest of anyone truly involved in the mental health field. Dr. Forrer points the beam of his elaborate curiosity into the darkest recesses of the preverbal mental processes. His book ranges wide in its explanations, discussions, and considerations of the vicissitudes of the weaning process. His concepts challenge some of the most cherished ideas in psychiatry, and since these ideas are cherished and have been learned at the cost of much energy and personal investment, the challenge will not go unheeded.

One of the most important things to be remembered about this book is that it does have vast clinical application. The theory, itself, is fascinating and provocative, but it might not be so if it were not applicable to the daily practice of psychiatry. Although Dr. Forrer arrives at conclusions which will certainly stimulate controversy in many areas of psychopathology, I believe that his discussion of schizophrenia will bring the pot to a boil. This is a refreshing chapter in these days of overemphasis upon biological and physio-chemical psychiatry, and all of the other attempts to classify all of the seriously mentally ill as having a disease almost devoid of the interpersonal process. Dr. Forrer's book adds fresh testimony to the ever-increasing body of evidence that psychopathology begins extremely early in the human organism, and that some fundamental processes are laid down and deeply ingrained long before the classical oedipal situation, or even long before the famous and infamous toilet training period.

It must be emphasized that this is a pioneering effort; that there are gaps in the theory; but that the overall formulation provides an exciting matrix from which a new concept of maturation might be developed. The reader of this work will once again be impressed with the fact that no scientific area ever is closed to new insights. No scientific law is unchangeable. No scientific concept is unalterable.

For those who feel or who have felt that psychiatric research must now confine itself to the biochemical laboratory, this work will provide a new stimulus for mitotic division of ideas and the fruitful multiplication of new beliefs. Psychiatry must not stand still and it must not become just another subspecialty of medicine. Psychological medicine can stand on its own and exhibit its body of knowledge to the world. Our image is not at issue. Reality must take our measure.

April 3, 1968

The above preface to *Weaning and Human Development* by Gordon R. Forrer, M.D., has been supplied by Sidney Bolter, M.D. Dr. Bolter is a Fellow of the American Psychiatric Association, a Diplomate of the American Board of Psychiatry and Neurology, formerly Director of Education at Northville State Hospital, and presently Medical Director of Kingswood Hospital, Detroit, Mich.

ACKNOWLEDGEMENT

The author appreciates the assistance above and beyond the demands of friendship of William C. Wiley, Associate Director, Bendix Laboratories. The efforts of S. A. Goudsmit of Brookhaven National Laboratory in the author's behalf are gratefully acknowledged.

CONTENTS

CONTENTS

CHAPTER I

The Oral Instinct

The oral instinct is the name given to those forces which function to provide the nutritional requirements of the organism. It is convenient to view the instinct as having both an *aim* and an *object*. The *aim* is to achieve satiation. The accomplishment of satiation is said to come about by the discharge of instinctual tension, a state of being that is experienced by the individual as uncomfortable. In the case of the oral instinct the instinctual tension is perceived as hunger. The *object* of the instinct is the medium through which the *aim* is to be achieved. In terms of the fundamental function of the oral instinct, that *object* is food. The executives of the oral instinct are those anatomical structures through which the *instinctual* aim, by means of their physiological activity, seek their *object*. A shorter but less precise way of saying it would be that the mouth serves as the means by which hunger is allayed. It is a rather remarkable and very significant fact that the organism is endowed with a quantity of oral instinctual energy considerably in excess of what would be required simply to insure nutrition. In contrast to the sexual instinct, where direct satisfaction serves no survival function for the individual, the oral instincts are imperative in their demands for satiation. The *aim* of the oral instinct is the incorporation of food. Once sufficient food has been incorporated to dispel the feelings of hunger, the excess of oral instinctual energy may be directed through other organs as further satiation, or discharge of oral instinctual tension is sought.

Certain organs lend themselves quite readily to this incorporative aim of the oral instinct. The eye, for example, takes in light through the pupil, ultimately registering

1

this fact in consciousness. The mind is "filled," as it were, with a scene. What we categorize as "curiosity" to see new sights and fresh vistas is really felt by some persons as a species of hunger. Indeed, the avidity with which people so often use their eyes to gratify themselves shows how much satisfaction there is to be gained through this particular incorporative activity. The ear also "takes in" sound, in turn transmitting it as nerve impulses through the N VIII until it is conducted by nerve pathways in the brain to the cerebral cortex, where the nerve impulses are sorted out and experienced as "sound." Language is replete with references to the "filling" effect of sound. Later on in this work the precise mechanism by which the function of hearing satisfies the demands of the oral instinct for satiation will be developed. As a matter of fact, it appears that any receptive sensory mechanism, be it seeing, hearing, smelling, tasting, feeling, touch, or pain, can and often does serve as the functional executive of the oral instinct.

Just as the primal *aim* of the oral instinct seeks its discharge through the various sensory organ systems of the body, so the primal *object* of the oral instinct may in similar fashion be displaced to other than nutritive substances. Thus, through looking, the eyes "take in" visual impressions, the ears "take in" sound, the nose incorporates odors, the skin, touch, and the pain receptors, pain. These various sensory systems come to serve as executives by which originally oral *aims* seek other than oral *objects*. When a stimulus is received by a receptor organ the resultant consciousness of this event fills, to some degree, one's awareness. Sometimes consciousness is so completely filled with sensation that there is room for little else. A sudden loud noise, a bee sting, a speck of dust in the eye are examples of sensory events that instantly wash away almost all other mental content. The same essential relationship is found in the original achievement of satiation of the oral instinct. The food (stimulus)

2

enters the mouth (receptor organ) and alleviates hunger tension (fills). It is because of this parallelism that the sensory apparatus of the body can serve an ancillary function assigned to it by the psyche. It can be said, I think without opposition, that any body function or any activity which contains a parallelism with the primal oral instinctual gratification (where the *aim* is to incorporate food) can be "drafted" by the psyche to serve oral functions concurrently with those which the organs serve in their own right.

There is a specificity to the oral instinct which limits its displacement of its incorporative *aim*. The sublimation of sexual instinctual energy is not limited by the rigid requirements of parallelism described above for the oral instincts. It is apparent that there are very great differences between those forces which preserve the individual and those which serve to propagate the race. Of the two instincts, the oral is, from embryological considerations, much the older. Nature devotes an abundance of care and concern to the early functional capabilities of the executive structures of the oral instinct. We can observe, in this connection, that the executives of the oral impulses are laid down embryologically even before sexual differentiation is detectable. By the 30th day after conception the rudimentary mouth and the organs accessory and complementary thereto—the eye, the ear, and the nose—are structurally present in the human embryo. In the XVI somite stage, the mandible and maxillary process are identifiable. But it is not until the third month after conception that the external genitalia are sufficiently developed to distinguish the sex of the fetus! This embryological sequence indicates that the instinct of which these organs are the executive holds first importance in the hierarchy of anatomical structures. Though oral strivings may be seemingly overshadowed by sexual ones in adult life, either instinctual aim may find expression in terms of the other.

3

The anatomical structures which serve the oral instinct develop concurrently with the heart, without which further embryological differentiation cannot proceed. Not only do the sensory organs innervated by cranial nerves make their appearance next, but functionally they serve to reinforce and improve the efficiency of the executive organ of the oral instinct—the mouth. It is instructive to think of the olfactory, auditory, and optic systems, as well as the limbs of the body, as organs which are adjunctive to the mouth and which altogether have interrelated, coordinated physiological functions, each serving in its specialized way as an executive of the oral instinct.

The oral instinct is backed up by an extremely elaborate support system. Evolution has determined that survival of the individual must be assured before propagation of the race can be considered. The mouth and those structures innervated by the cranial nerves—the eyes, ears, nose, tongue, cheek and upper gastrointestinal tract—are not only related to each other functionally but have interconnections through the central nervous system which make possible highly complex coordinated behavior at birth. Some organs which contribute executive functions supporting and promoting the oral instinctual aim are only partially developed at birth and must be successively "phased-in." Though the limbs are anatomically present, for example, they cannot serve as executives for the oral instinct until myelinization has made possible coordinated, purposeful movements. Once the upper extremities become "functional" they serve the oral instinct by bringing food to the mouth. Still later, when the legs become useful as a means of locomotion, they serve to bring the whole organism, if need be, to a food supply otherwise beyond reach. This successive "phasing-in" of ancillary supports for the execution of the oral instinctual aim of incorporation establishes an in-depth anatomical mechanism which is virtually unassailable.

If, for some reason, anomalous embryological development or accident interferes with one of the executives of the oral instinct—whether from the sensory side (Nerves I, II, V, VIII, IX, X and XII) or the motor side (Nerves III, IV, V, VI VII, IX X, XI and XII)—the nature of the anatomical-physiological linkages of one accessory organ with another makes possible the continued operation of at least some of the executives serving the oral instinct. There is, in addition, bilateral innervation and bilateral cortical representation of both sensory and motor sides of the accessory oral executives, a fact which one could say "overinsures" the capability of the organism to discharge its oral instinctive impulses. The embryological pattern described earlier is paralleled ontogenetically, for the oral functions are operative long before sexual manifestations are observable. It is almost as though the sexual instincts have not been coerced by the requirements of individual survival into the rigid psychophysiological framework within which the oral instincts must operate. Evolution assures the newborn that he will begin life endowed with an efficient physical capacity to suckle effectively. But even with the in-depth psychophysiological backup, it is only because forces outside himself see to it that the object of the infant's instinctual oral aim is achieved that the infant survives. As physical growth proceeds, the reflex sucking of objects touched to the lips is extinguished. It may reappear in severe functional regressive states as well as subsequent to destruction of brain tissue. A prominent libidinal component reinforces the powerful instinctual impulse to suck during infancy. During the course of the process of maturation this libidinal component becomes split off from the sucking reflex through a mechanism to be described. From the time of birth and for the first weeks of life, the libidinal gratification associated with sucking is easily observed and identified. I call this libidinal component of nursing *merging*. The *merging* undergoes modification as the infant matures, a subject to be dealt with in detail in later chapters.

CHAPTER II

The Hunger Tide

There are two basic rhythms displayed by the gastric musculature. The first is the "tonus rhythm," the fluctuations of which are not detectable without especially sensitive recording instruments. They are slow and quite constant with a frequency of up to three waves a minute. It is against this background of an almost invariant tonus rhythm that the much more evident hunger contractions occur. They arise as forceful peristaltic waves in the cardia of the stomach; the entire stomach musculature becomes involved in the contractions. They are episodic—beginning some three hours after a meal—quite possibly in response to the fact that after this period of time the stomach has been almost completely emptied by the movement of its contents into the duodenum and beyond. The hunger contractions, already noted to be episodic, endure for a few minutes to as long as an hour and a half. These periods of contraction are separated from each other by varying intervals when, save for the ever-present gastric tonus rhythm, the stomach is quiescent. This period of quiescence may be as short as half an hour or as long as two and a half hours. There is a correlation between the hunger contractions and the conscious awareness of the sensation of hunger. It seems generally true that the more forceful the hunger contractions, the more intense the sensations of hunger.

The hunger waves build up in intensity, achieving a maximum at about the midpoint of the contraction period. From that point onward they decrease until gastric quiescence is established. At the same time their frequency gradually increases. At their commencement the waves

6

occur several minutes apart, the frequency increasing so that toward the end of this phase of gastric activity the contractions are almost continuous, so rapidly does each follow the one preceding it. The tetanic-like muscular activity may persist as long as 15 minutes, but usually has a duration of under five minutes. As might be expected from the established relationship between hunger contractions and the sensation of hunger, the phase of virtually continuous massive contraction is associated with the type of pain we commonly call "hunger pangs." As people age, this particular physiological feature diminishes and is unusual in those who have passed their youth. Both hunger contractions and the constant background of the gastric tonus rhythm have been found in infants immediately after birth. It has been further shown that the sleeping infant awakes and cries when the hunger waves have become established and are increasing in tempo.

It would seem logical, in view of the occurrence of hunger every three or four hours, that the eating customs of mankind cluster around such time intervals or multiples thereof. This is sometimes the case, but there is wide variation in practice. Among the Aborigines of Australia, whose food supplies are uncertain and unpredictable, the availability of food determines when and in what amounts it will be consumed. One reads accounts of enormous amounts of food being eaten at one sitting—presumably because the Aborigine never knows when next he will eat and hence has to take advantage of food whenever the occasion offers. In contrast, among the Eskimo food is generally available—seal or fish either freshly caught or cached previously in anticipation of need. As among the Australian Aborigine, there is no regularity of mealtime, but for a different reason. The Eskimo eat on the basis of whim or instant desire. They have no schedule in their living arrangements. If the notion seizes them, they may stop in the middle of a blizzard while on their way from one village to another, unpack their sleds and prepare a meal when, by waiting half an hour, all could have been accomplished much more comfortably indoors and out of the storm. Members of hunting cultures frequently down enormous quantities of meat from a successful hunt. They live in a feast-or-famine civilization with little regularity to their mealtimes. Not only is there great variation in the timing of meals, but the type of food consumed varies from culture to culture. The exclusive fat and meat protein of the Eskimo contrasts strikingly with the almost exclusive carbohydrate diet of Asian groups, for example. The obsessive concern of the modern American for a balanced diet is a modern folkway, made possible by readily available food, abundant in variety and quantity, and an almost total absence of significant taboos and religious regulations regarding what may and may not be consumed.

Although the dietary habits and customs of adults vary extensively, every infant suckles milk from birth. His diet is the same regardless of the culture into which he is born. Except for the introduction of small amounts of other edibles., infants feed on milk at least through the conclusion of the *weaning process*. In some cultural settings milk is a dietary staple and continues to be consumed long after weaning is completed. The source of the milk is of no known great psychological moment, and if the custom in many American homes to bottle-feed a milk formula rather than to breast-feed has effect upon the infant, this is presently unrecognized. The matter, however, requires more investigation. When it comes to the nursing of an infant, one encounters a two-person transaction having complex ramifications, some of which we shall presently study.

It is not until the weaning process has been accomplished that an individual's dietary habits and customs begin to assume the configuration of the culture into which he has been born. It is self-evident that no matter what course the dietary habits, customs, and necessities of people take, at the beginning of their lives all obtain nourishment through suckling. All have an oral instinct seeking discharge through psychophysiological mechanisms, about which little is presently known. There is no reason to believe that this particular feature of infant behavior is any different today than it was ten million years ago. They eat according to an *"Infantile Mode"* which is readily distinguishable from the *"Adult Mode."* The *"Weaning Process"* is the sum of the sequence of steps taken in passing from the *"Infantile Mode"* to the *"Adult Mode"* of behavior. Further details will be explored later.

We must first investigate the physiology of sucking and thoroughly inform ourselves on the facts thereof. For any psychological proposal must, in my judgment, be solidly grounded in physiology. I have employed known physiological facts, but linking them in a meaningful manner has required semantic inventions, several of which have already been introduced.

The term "Hunger Tide" designates the ebb and flow of the awareness of hunger, the psychic representation of the already described hunger contractions of the stomach. Though the mechanism by which the hunger contractions wax and wane is not well understood, we do know that the eating of food or the placing of nutriments in the stomach has a profound and immediate influence on the hunger contractions. As a consequence of their lessening, the sensation of hunger disappears, to be replaced by the awareness of a feeling of satiation.

Anyone can confirm the existence of the *Hunger Tide.* If, for example, one misses lunch usually eaten at noon and the opportunity to eat comes, let us say, at 2 p.m., one often finds that at this later time he is not hungry! Logically, such a person should be quite hungry, for he has gone without food for a longer than usual time. Curiously, his appetite has either decreased or disappeared. What has happened, of course, is that the *Hunger Tide,* having

9

reached its high point at lunch time, has subsequently entered its ebb phase, a reflection of the physiological decrease of the hunger contractions which, having progressively lessened during the interval of time between lunch and 2 P.M., have achieved the quiescent stage. The very nature of gastric physiology determines that the sensation of hunger will wane and even disappear despite the fact that food has not been eaten. Of course, with the passage of time the physiological hunger contractions recommence in the cardia of the stomach and as before spread to embrace the entire stomach musculature. When this happens the subjective awareness of hunger is awakened not infrequently with an increase in intensity. If food is withheld for a further period, the *Hunger Tide* continues to ebb and flow, a state of hunger alternating with a state of nonhunger. Of course, when the experiment is carried to extremes and long periods of time intervene between feedings, or when the feedings are scanty and physiologically insufficient, the *Hunger Tide* is modified and the hunger pangs become increasingly uncomfortable and almost, if not entirely, continuous.

The pattern of ebb and flow of the sensation of hunger comes to assume a psychological significance in our lives that has gone unrecorded and unrecognized. Though we do not become consciously aware of the periodicity of the *Hunger Tide* until we are well past infancy, the hunger contraction cycle which it reflects is a physiological one already inextricably rooted in the patterns and rhythms of bodily functions at the time of birth. Experience suggests that there are individual variations in the intensity and degree of perception of the hunger pangs accompanying the contractions of the gastric musculature. There also appear to be individual patterns of fluctuations in the periodicity of the peaks and valleys of the *Hunger Tide,* so that while we consider the psychophysiology of the gastrointestinal tract in general, we must not neglect the existence of individual variations, the ultimate significance of which are presently unknown. It hardly needs saying, of course, that the entry of food into the stomach interrupts sensation of hunger. When food is eaten the hunger contractions, if present, immediately become quiescent and the appetite—a psychic reflection of the physiological alterations which the food has produced in the stomach—decreases.

Not long ago an eleven-year-old boy asked me a question which puzzled him. "Why is it," he asked, "when I'm hungry at suppertime and I eat just a little bit, that I lose my appetite? I was real hungry when I sat down but I just ate a little bit and then I wasn't hungry like I was." The explanation, of course, lies in the fact that just prior to supper his hunger contractions were both frequent and vigorous. This was reflected in his awareness of the peak of the *Hunger Tide*. The food he ate in small amounts produced a physiological decrease in the gastric contractions. In terms of the *Hunger Tide* there had been a rapid ebb brought about by food entering his stomach. This is what lay behind the child's observation that once he had eaten "a little bit" he was no longer as hungry as he had been. The *Hunger Tide* ebbs and flows with a rhythmicity that reflects the delicate psychophysiological mechanism through which food requirements are determined without our conscious participation. When we analyze the *Hunger Tide* phenomenon in infants we learn that an especially deep and inextricable interrelationship exists between psychic and physiological functioning.

Since the infant cannot communicate verbally what he perceives, the investigator must rely on his observations of the effects of the ebb and flow of the *Hunger Tide*. Some are measurable physiological ones. For example, infants become hungry every three and a half to four hours and signal the fact by crying for food. The well-known four-hour feeding intervals so often prescribed for infants take advantage of this physiologically based hunger cycle. The accompanying Graph # I illustrates the *Hunger*

11

Tide. Time is indicated along the abscissa. The intensity of the hunger contractions in the stomach is represented along the ordinate. The dotted line above and parallel to the abscissa represents the hunger threshold. When the gastric contractions reach a force of sufficient intensity this threshold is reached (at "A" in the graph) and the infant perceives the sensation of hunger. With the passage of more time this sensation increases in intensity, reaching its maximum at point "B." Between "B" and "C" hunger has lessened but is still perceived. The perception ceases as the *Hunger Tide* passes below the hunger threshold at point "C." From "C" to "D" the contractions become increasingly less intense until quiescence is achieved at "D." As already noted, not all infants have such a rigid four-hour cycle as shown in this illustration. Moreover, there is considerable variation in the frequency of the *Hunger Tide* in individual infants. All that really can be said is that the cyclic appearance of hunger clusters about a time interval of four hours. One can observe that physical illness disrupts the *Hunger Tide,* but very little beyond this is known in regard to the effects various psychophysiological influences may have upon it.

In Graph #2 I have shown schematically what is experienced in relationship to the *Hunger Tide* by an infant who, for the purposes of illustration, is not fed. Let's assume that the child, three weeks old, has initially been fed so that he is fully satiated. The hunger pangs increase with the passage of time until at point "A" they exceed the threshold of hunger—an event signaled by the infant's cry. This response to the discomfort produced by the hunger contractions persists until after the *Hunger Tide* has first reached its maximum at "B" and has then decreased in intensity to where it no longer exceeds the hunger threshold indicated by point "C." The infant now falls asleep, a reaction we traditionally ascribe to his having "tired himself out with his crying." After a further lapse of time during which the infant has been asleep, the *Hunger Tide*

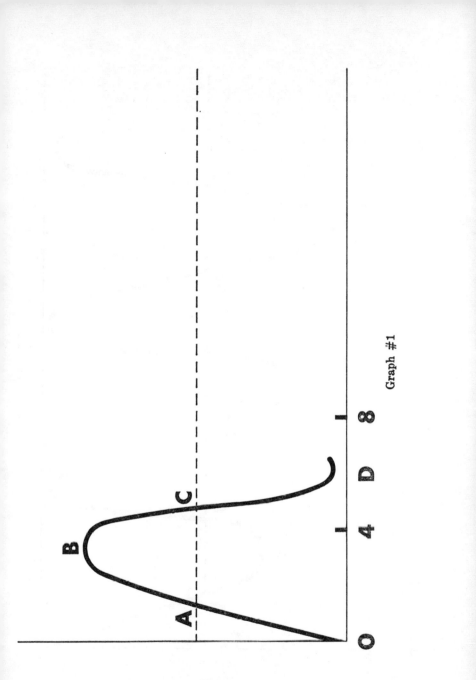

Graph #1

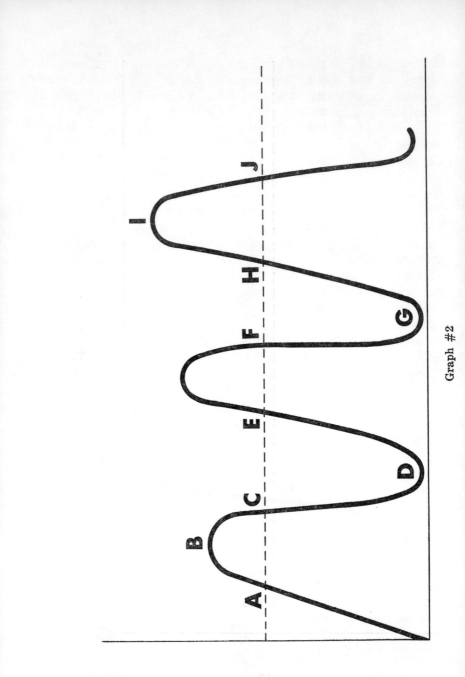

Graph #2

14

has reached "D," passed through the quiescent stage, and begins to flow again. The hunger contractions gradually increase in intensity and frequency until once more the threshold of hunger is exceeded where indicated by point "E." Once more the infant's behavior reflects the physiological events transpiring in his stomach. He cries in hunger and continues to cry. The crying tapers off as the intensity of the hunger contractions decrease. When the discomfort he has been experiencing declines sufficiently in intensity so that it is not painful, he ceases to cry. On the graph this occurs at point "F." Once more the infant sleeps. The *Hunger Tide* continues to ebb still further below the hunger perception threshold. The curve approaches "G" where the gastric contractions again become quiescent. Again the *Hunger Tide* flows, passing through the hunger perception threshold at "H" and rising to an even greater maximum of discomfort at "I." This latter point corresponds to the near tetanic muscular contractions of the entire stomach described earlier. With time these contractions decrease in intensity and frequency and the *Hunger Tide* ebbs until at "J" the pangs of hunger are no longer felt as the intensity of the gastric contractions falls below the hunger perception threshold once more. Again the infant falls asleep. By painstaking examination of this cyclic event we discover an interesting fact. The infant fell asleep on the ebb of the *Hunger Tide* because, as the hunger sensations decreased, the psychophysiological situation became like that which exists after the infant has been fed. Namely, the stomach musculature becomes quiescent.

How does this matter appear when viewed from the position of the infant? He of course cannot conceptualize as we can, nor has he any words to think with, nor even much experience applicable to the various situations that present themselves. By employing the data available, even if in the past some of this was disregarded as immaterial, perhaps we can formulate a meaningful and probable theory.

We must try to arrive at reasonable and logical conclusions and at the same time stay within the infant's limitations of perception and understanding.

The infant whose *Hunger Tide* was indicated on Graph #2 did not *know* he was hungry. His ego was not sufficiently developed to distinguish self from nonself. He cried reflexly in response to the discomfort which was perceived via the sensory limb of his nervous system. Let us return to the graph. It has been pointed out how his *Hunger Tide* flows until at point "A" its intensity exceeds the hunger threshold and he starts crying. Moreover, he continues to do so until point "C" is reached when, because the intensity of hunger is less than the hunger threshold, he falls asleep. I pause in my discussion to bring to the reader's attention an experience of the infant not previously commented upon. The infant perceives among other auditory stimuli the *sound of his own cry*. Moreover, even as he cries his discomfort diminishes and at "C" disappears altogether. He falls asleep when the *Hunger Tide* ebbs and the hunger pangs disappear, just as he would have fallen asleep, had the hunger pangs been relieved by milk! The means by which he experienced the pleasure of no longer being the subject of the painful awareness of hunger is of no concern to the infant. His ego has hardly begun to differentiate. Early in infancy attention is directed to sensory perceptions, not to the means by which these manifestations are produced.

The very primitive relationship where the environment has not yet been differentiated from the self exists for a short time. Very soon after birth the ego begins to develop and promptly commences to "learn." It begins to compare sensory experiences, one with another, and to associate events occurring in close temporal relationship. All events producing identical perceptions are naturally equated one with the other at this early phase of ego development. Thus, no significance is attached by the infant during the first weeks of life to the person who feeds him. It is simply beyond his perceptual capacity to recognize either his own or others' individuality. Nor can one observe in the early weeks that it makes any difference to the infant whether the bottle contains goat's, mare's or mother's milk. Nor even, according to one piece research, is it of any moment whether the bottle contents be warm or cold. Accordingly, I think it unlikely that there is any distinction between hunger sensation terminated by nursing and hunger pangs disappearing as a consequence of the ebb of the *Hunger Tide* as described. What the infant "knows" is that for whatever reason he no longer experiences the discomfort of hunger. A physiological basis for the disappearance of hunger, whether or not the infant be fed, has been demonstrated. This is reflected at the clinical level by the observation that in both instances the infant ceases to cry and goes to sleep.

As the ego gradually extends the compass of its own boundaries it develops the capacity to store for later recall what it experiences, and the associations related thereto. A precise age at which this process begins cannot be given, but a primitive memory is established within the first few months of life. When the infant experiences something of which he has never before been cognizant, he compares the new event with what he already "knows"—he "understands" the new event in terms of what is already known—after which this understanding of the new experience is itself stored in the memory bank. Henceforth it will serve as one more memory to be retrieved for purposes of comparison when the unfamiliar is next encountered. The acquisition of speech accelerates the learning and memory process many times since the memory bank can then be supplied with more versatile verbal symbols.

In addition to the learning process as described, a related capability is developed by the ego. The latter commences to "associate" events which occur in temporal relationship to each other. The concept of "etiology" is, early in life, a very simple one. "A" occurs when "B" does, therefore the two are associated in the psyche. And when "A" occurs in temporal proximity to "B", the infant concludes that "A" causes "B." (This primitive theory of causality often persists throughout life and is a basis for superstition, delusion, and manifestations of credulity.)

I shall go into this matter more fully in a subsequent chapter. At this time I would merely bring to the reader's attention such an association, one that has far-reaching implications for theoretical and clinical psychiatry. As the infant cries, it has been emphasized, he *perceives his own cry.* As a matter of fact, he cannot fail to do so both by air and bone conduction from the moment of birth. When he is not fed and he cries in hunger and discovers that his hunger recedes nonetheless, he associates the "cry" (which his immature ego cannot yet grasp belongs to himself) with the disappearance of his hunger.

Graph #3 follows the same general form as the previous ones. The dotted line parallel to the abscissa, as before, represents the awareness of hunger sensations. The hatched area of the graph which lies above the hunger threshold reminds us that the infant is crying during this period. Now let us examine the effect of food on the *Hunger Tide.* At point "A" the infant is offered the breast and the moment he begins to suckle the hunger contractions decrease both in frequency and intensity and the stomach musculature achieves a state of quiescence. (It is to be noted that an infant crying vigorously in hunger is too preoccupied with the whole experience to take breast or bottle even when offered, so that his attention must be called to the fact that food is available by means of greater than customary stimulation of the sucking reflex.) Once the infant's hunger has been satiated he sleeps. The *Hunger Tide* is, of course, not permanently dampened by the feeding. For approximately four hours it has waxed strongly enough to have broken through the hunger perception barrier at "B." The stomach has mean-

18

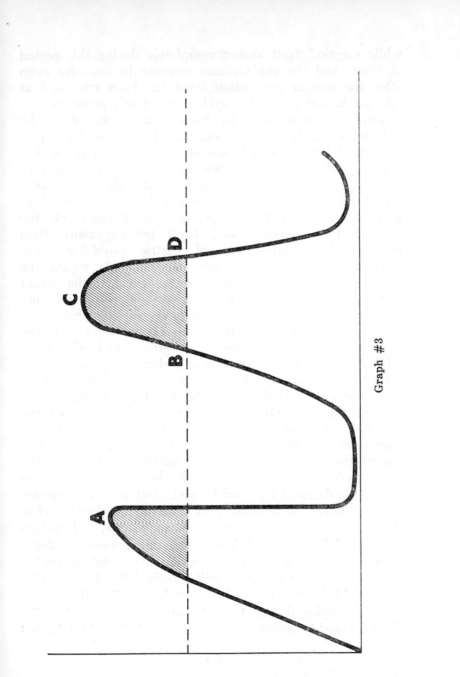

Graph #3

while emptied itself almost completely during this period of time. And the contractions increase in intensity even after the hunger perception level has been exceeded at "B." As in the preceding cycle the infant's perception of discomfort is announced by the cry, as indicated by the hatched area. The infant continues to cry until his perception of hunger, which has begun to ebb at point "C," reaches point "D," at which moment the sensation of hunger is no longer perceivable. Naturally the infant's crying ceases since it commenced and was maintained as a reflex response to hunger pangs. Because of the ebb of the *Hunger Tide,* itself nothing more than the psychic manifestation of gastric physiology, the discomfort ceases. The hunger stimulus (to which the cry is a response) no longer being present, the infant stops crying. The state of affairs just described does not remain static. As the infant matures physiologically and psychologically, the primitive reflex cry in response to the perception of hunger becomes progressively modified. In adulthood, for example, one may endure the pain and discomfort of starvation without so much as shedding a tear.

I have emphasized the fundamental physiological pattern of the stomach musculature and demonstrated the correlation of psychological responses with physiological phenomena in the stomach and elsewhere. I have discussed the influence of food on gastric rhythm and the psychological consequences of the hunger tide, whether or not the demand for food be met. And most importantly I have shown the possibility of error in the popular view that an infant, crying in response to hunger, falls asleep because of "exhaustion." There is a much more satisfying answer to the puzzling question of why an infant, crying in hunger at one moment, will shortly fall asleep despite the fact his hunger pangs have not been relieved by food! I have employed the term *"Hunger Tide"* to describe the relationship between perception and the physiological rhythmicity of gastric contractions. By correlating what is demonstrable physiologically with what is observable behavior in the infant, I have come to the conclusion that areas of the psychophysiology of infancy, now considered settled questions, must be reopened for further investigation.

A mother's response to her hungry infant when studied in detail can be shown to be uniquely tailored for that child. Even the most superficial observations reveal striking differences of maternal response. Some react only after an infant's hunger cry is undeniable. Others offer breast or bottle at the slightest whimper. There are those who try to anticipate and offer food early during the ascendant portion of the *Hunger Tide*. An infant may be offered milk at the convenience of a mother who pays no particular heed to his state of desire for food. Some do and some do not breast-feed. There is hardly an end to the matter, of course, when detailed differences are considered. It cannot be to the nursing infant is of no great moment. Despite the conceded that the quality and pattern of maternal response classificatory difficulties presented by such a vast array of possible maternal reactions to the hunger of nursing infants, I think a model can be constructed which will, in a general way, convey an understanding of the basic response of the infant to the events experienced while he is a nursling.

One must suppose that most mothers the world over respond to the nursling with at least some uniformity. The infant signals his hunger by his cry and the mother naturally responds to this by presenting him with breast or bottle. And generally, during the earliest days after birth, this cycle is repeated at approximately four-hour intervals as a reflection of the *Hunger Tide*. Inevitably, there is some lag between the first moment of perception of hunger by the infant, communicated to the world by his cry, and the satiation of his emptiness by nursing. It is furthermore obvious that the time lag between the infant's signal of

21

hunger and the satiation thereof varies from one occasion to the next and is, in considerable measure, dependent upon the individual attitude of the mother as well as the technique she follows in feeling her infant. If, for example, the infant resides in a cultural setting which accepts the nursing of infants in the presence of adults, it is likely, all things being equal, that there will be very little time lag between the infant's first cry of hunger and the offering of the breast. But if there is some inhibition or embarrassment about nursing in public and the mother must seek isolation to perform this function, then some time must be spent in seeking privacy prior to suckling the infant. Should the infant be fed by bottle instead of by breast, it is obvious that an even greater time lag will develop between the onset of hunger and its satiation. For when the infant is fed by bottle, the milk, by long tradition, must first be heated; a procedure which delays the infant's satiation and requires him to experience for a longer time and to a greater extent the discomfort of hunger pangs.

Although, generally speaking, the feeding cycle corresponds with the rise and fall of the *Hunger Tide,* it often happens that such is not always possible. One rather imagines that in infancy an occasional discordance occurs but this, I should think, would in most instances be exceptional. There is a very popular system of feeding infants which rather remarkably puts aside the desires of the infant as unworthy of consideration. The four-hour feeding schedule may be physiological insofar as the time interval between the peaks of the infant's hunger contractions are concerned, but it neglects entirely both the individual character of each infant's *Hunger Tide* and what, at this point, we have presumed is the desirability of the feeding cycle corresponding to the hunger cycle. It seems likely that what subsequently we shall discuss as an ill-advised technique for feeding infants has had its potentially damaging effects minimized by a natural tendency of mothers to listen to their infants with more attention than they render to the prescribing physician. Where the four-hour feeding schedule is slavishly adhered to, as sometimes happens, the simple, logical and natural relationship between the need for food and and the satisfaction of hunger can become completely disordered. There is abundant clinical evidence that there are aftereffects persisting throughout life as a consequence of discordancies arising in the very earliest time of life. For even on first inspection one observes that when the infant is fed on a schedule predetermined for him rather than because he is hungry, the expected association between hunger and suckling and satiation becomes distorted. Under the four-hour plan the infant has to be fed every four hours regardless of the state of his appetite! As a result, milk may be offered when the infant is not hungry—that is to say, when the gastric hunger contractions are in a quiescent phase. And, by the same token, milk may be withheld when the hunger contractions are at their height. Furthermore, the resultant phase-discordancy between the *Hunger Tide* and the feeding cycle tends to be inconstant, so that from the infant's point of view an uncertainty of association between the sensation of hunger and relief of that hunger by food inevitably arises.

One can understand how this may come about by considering Graph #4. This graph demonstrates the effect of the imposition of a four-hour feeding schedule on the infant. The four-hour intervals are indicated along the abscissa. Each four hours quiescence of the stomach musculature takes place regardless of the phase of the hunger curve. The line above and parallel to the abscissa indicates, as on the preceding graphs the hunger threshold. At the beginning we consider the infant fed and the hunger contractions quiescent. Starting then from zero time, the *Hunger Tide* waxes until it reaches and exceeds the hunger threshold. At this point the infant begins to cry indicated by the hatched areas. It so happens that

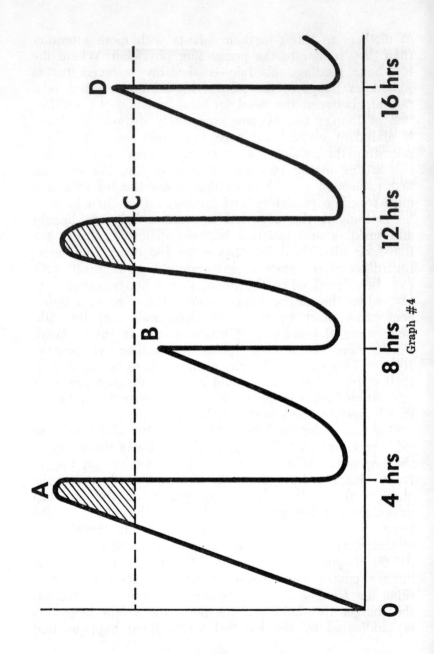

Graph #4

just as the *Hunger Tide* reaches its apex at "A," four hours has elapsed since zero time, and the infant is fed. The gastric contractions promptly respond by becoming quiescent and, as indicated, the infant ceases to feel hunger. After a period of quiescence the gastric contractions begin again their progressive increase in frequency and intensity as the *Hunger Tide* waxes. The hunger pangs have not yet reached the hunger threshold, but since the time for the next feeding has arrived, it now being the eighth hour, the infant is fed at "B." That is to say, he is "forced" to eat even though he has no sensation of hunger. As noted, the flowing *Hunger Tide* promptly subsides as quiescence of the gastric musculature supervenes. Once again the *Hunger Tide* begins to rise. And here, because of the variations in frequency of the *Hunger Tide,* it happens that the hunger threshold is exceeded and the *Hunger Tide* reaches its apogee. Despite the fact the infant has been crying since the hunger threshold was breeched, food is withheld until the 12th hour, at which moment the hunger sensations, though still perceived by the infant, are nevertheless beginning to wane. At "C" the infant is fed with the now familiar result that the *Hunger Tide* ebbs as the gastric musculature becomes quiescent. At the sixteenth hour feeding it happens that the *Hunger Tide* has just barely become sufficiently intense to be perceived as hunger. At "D," just as the infant begins to cry, he is fed; the hunger contractions respond physiologically by the stomach becoming quiescent. The infant, because of his budding awareness—so limited as to hardly merit the designation of "understanding"—is the more readily confused by associations which do not consistently follow established patterns of relationship. It is only as maturity ripens—indeed, it is the sine qua non of psychological maturity—that the capacity to exercise judgments based upon considerations of relevance and appropriateness is achieved.

A feeding schedule which emphasizes a constant time

lapse between feedings, if rigidly adhered to, establishes conditions highly favorable for the cultivation of emotional uncertainty and confusion. In my experience those disturbed people who cannot define what they feel and hence frequently conduct their lives according to invariant rules, often were fed as infants at their mother's convenience rather than according to their own demands for food. Where from the time of birth a sequential relationship between the peak of the *Hunger Tide* and nursing is persistently maintained, the conception of the validity of one's own perceptions is enhanced. It seems basic "common sense" that one would "know" when he is hungry, but in actual fact there are those who cannot accurately assess their own sensory perceptions. In clinical psychiatry the physician frequently encounters patients who do not really know what they feel and who, on this account, are unable to acknowledge the validity of their own inner lives. As a consequence of not being capable of knowing with unassailable certainty what they feel, they live shallow and credulous lives. This pathological state arises from incoherence produced when the early conditioning to the aforementioned natural sequence of cause and effect between hunger and satiation has been significantly and persistently distorted. In brief then, the instinctual inclination of the mother to respond to the demands of her infant, to pay particular attention to his hunger cry, to nurse him and thereby relieve his pain, and to be pleased with what she accomplishes, normally establishes the infant's "position" in regard to himself. This is the period of life when the foundations of the psyche are being established. Whatever the direction psychological growth takes at the beginning of life, it is subsequently reinforced at many levels of experience. It should be clear that any imperfections of correlation between the sensory component of hunger and satiation are relative. The very nature of the relationship between the hunger and the feeding cycle makes it so. It is the occurrence of a persistent and habitual dissonance between the infant's perception of hunger and the nursing cycle that disrupts the formation of relevant association.

It would seem, despite what has been said, that discordance or time lag between the awareness of hunger and its satiation has an essential role to play in ego development. Hunger is obviously not the only experience which, by impinging on the infant's sensory receptors, alters feeling tone, but it does seem to be the first sensory experience identified by the ego. I have already suggested that a primitive, naïve kind of nonverbal reasoning arises in relationship to the experience of hunger being relieved as one suckles. In effect, the infant tries to discover the basis for whatever discordancies may occur between the *Hunger Tide* and the feeding cycle. That is to say, he develops a "theory" as to why he gets milk when he does and why, when the discomfort of hunger arises, he does not at that very moment obtain that which relieves it. "Speculation" as to why the hunger pangs disappear, even when they do so purely because of the cyclic *Hunger Tide*, also occurs. (The implications of this particular "infantile theory" will be dealt with in detail in a subsequent chapter.) The developing ego thus begins in simple, crude, and unsophisticated nonverbal terms to formulate infantile "theories" to explain the phenomena encountered and perceived. The infant takes a megalomanic position in regard to his personal world. His infantile "theories" are formulated on his basic assumption that every phenomenon encountered has an etiological relationship with himself! It is difficult, of course, to conceive of a mere infant in arms conducting any significant mentation. Indeed, only the earliest rudiments of "thinking," as we adults know the term, are present in the early months of life. The capacity to associate one event with another is developed quite early. For example, an infant will cease crying, if not too hungry, just at the sight of its bottle. His sight being "filled" with the milk probably has an immediate quiescent effect on the hunger pangs.

When I write of "theories" I employ the term advisedly, there simply being no other way to articulate the matter. In accordance with the infant's megalomanic position, he relates all that he perceives through his sensory receptors as arising on account of some action, attitude, or fantasy of his own. His capacity to test reality is tenuous and hardly can be said to exist within the small compass of what he conceptualizes to be the universe. The earliest occurrence of magical thinking is concerned entirely with the associations established between hunger and its relief, but later it comes to embrace other aspects of living as well. Depending upon his experience with events naturally associated with each other, he inevitably arrives at the conclusion that he is the prime mover within his universe. Of course, these early impressions are later corrected by the ego when reality-testing becomes firmly established as the modus operandi of the ego. But in the early weeks and months, time related associations form the basis from which "infantile theory" is built. A host of fascinating and important questions arise in this connection.

How does the time lag factor between two events influence the association of the two events in the psyche? Consider again the sequence of sensation-of-hunger, hunger-cry, nursing, and satiation. Because of the close association of each with the other it can be seen that the infant may "theorize" that he is fed because he cries. Accordingly he may attribute magical properties to the sound of his own voice. We do not learn of this association directly from infants, of course, since they do not have the capability of articulating such conceptions. The circumstances preventing direct knowledge forces us to seek understanding through the analysis of clinical symptomatology perhaps years after its origin.

Consider, for example, a person loudly and indiscriminately complaining of some functional difficulty. The behavior he displays is incomprehensible save in terms of an "infantile theory" that if one cries out with sufficient volume then an inner need will be met and the discomfort will be alleviated. This analysis is supported by the fact that such patients invariably demand either overtly or by implication that the doctor "give them something." They care not what the cause of their discomfort may be nor have they the remotest idea of what might be done by themselves to relieve it. They credit without question the power of the doctor to relieve them, and insist he give them medicine without so much as a pause to establish a diagnosis. They do not seek the "causes" of their difficulty and have no interest, usually, in a therapeutic method that offers more than symptomatic relief. They demand "results" and are annoyed and frustrated when these are not forthcoming immediately. They want someone else to relieve them and cannot grasp the idea of participating in this by helping themselves. Evidently this conception is so deeply rooted in the psyche because what is presently believed by them was a real experience during infancy. Some mothers "treat" all manner of discomfort by the simple expedient of nursing the complaining infant.

A woman patient of mine is attached to her mother by incredibly durable and persistent bonds. Mother and daughter have developed between themselves a system of private communication. They communicate by saying what, on the surface, appears to be one thing while at a deeper level an opposite meaning is implied. The daughter says to her mother, for example, that she has not been able to visit her for a few days because she has been busy with other activities. The mother replies that such behavior on her daughter's part is perfectly understandable. But the tone of her voice and the expression on her face presents her daughter with an impression not conveyed by her words. The patient understand the intended reproach and when her mother mentions how badly she has been feeling of late and relates that a neighbor has recently had a heart attack, the patient interprets this as a prediction of what will befall her mother because of her neglect to visit her daily! Sometimes the communication is not so subtly conveyed; the mother openly accuses the patient of causing her pain and illness by her independent behavior and lack of attentiveness.

When she first sought help the patient did not have any idea that she harbored, in her unconscious, negative feelings towards her mother. So intense was her dependency and her fear of her own impulses that she could not permit them to reach consciousness. Her attitude and behavior was based on the "infantile theory" that love and compliance was the price one had to pay for being fed. She became ill, it is interesting to note, when her mother, for reasons unconnected with the patient, began to withhold some of her accustomed attentiveness. When this occurred the patient became obsessed with ideas that her mother would suffer some terrible disease or mishap which would be directly attributable to herself.

One of her symptoms was the obsession that she had cancer of the rectum an idea secondary to somatic hallucinations she experienced in the area. This obsession expanded. She was certain she was about to die, that cancer had invaded every part of her body, that she should kill her husband so as not to be lonely in death. She had complained to many physicians, and their interest and attention to her complaints always produced a temporary remission of her obsessions. But a few days after each consultation they would return and she would revert to tears and "begging for help" (the expression she employed to describe her appeals to physicians). The curious manner of expression was quite puzzling because no one, including the patient, could define the "help" she avowedly sought. She operated on the theory that there was something a physician—or *somebody*—could do or say that could be of "help." From the point of view of "infantile theory" the problem of attaining that "help" was more specifically a problem of developing an appeal so that "help" would be elicited from someone.

Initially she demanded medication. I refused to comply, explaining that any tranquilizing medication I might prescribe would only make her feel worse. I assured her I had no intention of adding to her difficulties! Any medicine I might have given her would have provided instant but temporary relief. And this demonstration of my "magic" powers would have spoiled any possibility for successful psychotherapy. The patient's reasoning is that if the doctor, demonstrates his power to provide some relief by means of medication, he must have still more effective methods of treatment at his command. The patient is naturally disappointed and angry when his subsequent demands are unanswered. He either spends all his energies trying to extract further benefit from the doctor or leaves him for another. Accordingly, had I prescribed medication my patient would have come to expect ever greater benefits via "medicine" and implied assurance that she could be significantly helped by a means other than that which I had proposed, i.e., psychotherapy. If one keeps in mind that at one time in the patient's life there had been a product which, when taken by mouth, had relieved discomfort, it becomes clear that the patient's "theory" is far from irrelevant. Her covert position is that her condition is relievable. Accordingly, she need only find the right plea—the long "lost chord," as it were—to symbolically evoke in the present what was, during infancy, actually forthcoming when she cried out in discomfort.

The tendency of the ego to seek explanations that I label "infantile theory" has important bearing on all of one's subsequent psychological development. The tendency itself seems to be a manifestation conforming to a "law" of the conservation of psychic energy. An examination of

31

ego development suggests that reality-testing is achieved by the formulation of a succession of "theories" which attempt, in an economical way, to relate new experiences with associations already established in the psyche. As one "theory" proves untenable, a more satisfactory one takes its place and is itself replaced by a third as soon as its inadequacy has been discovered, and so on. Because each theory is a product of the individual's ego, it shares in the self-centeredness or narcissism which characterizes infantile ego. When, as sometimes happens, the process of theory formation and replacement becomes fixed at some particular level during infancy, psychopathological manifestations are inevitable in adult life. Superstition and belief in the miraculous are generally categories of credulousness traceable to a stage of "infantile theory." The following clinical example is illustrative.

A patient of mine was pregnant. Her six-year-old son asked her how the baby would be born. The mother, instead of replying immediately, had the wisdom and interest to ask her son, "You tell me how you think a baby is born." To this invitation the child replied questioningly, "From your rectum?" "No," the mother said. "From your breast?" the child continued. "No," the mother answered. "From your belly button?" he suggested. At this point the mother, not caring to explore further the powers of her son's imagination, told him how the infant she was carrying would be delivered. We observe how the child struggled with one unsatisfactory "theory" after another until the truth was finally learned. This particular case illustrates yet another significant psychological fact namely, that to young children *nothing* is impossible. As a result "infantile theories" frequently seem unthinkable, incredible, or amusing to adults who have forgotten how they once had to "figure out" the world at a time of life when they were in a position of well-nigh absolute ignorance of reality.

When the feeding cycle is consistently related to the

32

Hunger Tide it is very obvious that the infant quickly discovers the correct "theory" of how he obtains milk which relieves his hunger. From his point of view or "position" he formulates the tenable theory that because he cried when hungry, he is presented with milk. The first lesson in reality-testing has been learned! There is no confusion here, no wonderment, no distortion of the cause-effect relationship. This, of course, is but one of the possibilities, for when the conditions of consistency are absent, infantile theories are developed which lead away from rather than toward reality.

The young infant's "psyche" is dominated by the ebb and flow of his hunger sensations. Infantile theory formation which commences in relationship to the *Hunger Tide* is, at first, apparently structured quite simply. But as the ego develops, as an increasing number of associations become available for comparison with newly encountered perceptions, it becomes more complex while at the same time holding to the already established principle that temporal proximity indicates causality. Symbolic equivalence develops, based on the principle that if both "A" and "B" are the symbolic equivalent of "C," then "A" can be equated with "B."

As the infant matures, his threshold for the discomfort of hunger seems to rise so that if asleep he may remain so through periods of gastric activity of an intensity which earlier in his life would have awakened him. The commonplace early morning wakening for a feeding seems in some instances to be revived as a behavioral pattern under certain pathological states in later life. Persons suffering from depression, for example, frequently complain of awaking during the early morning hours. Characteristically, they remain abed, filled with what is best described as relatively contentless rumination. If the physician can persuade such sufferers to rise, prepare and consume a cup of hot milk and then return to bed, sleep often comes again. There is a curious predilection for this ruminative activity, and a good deal of resistance is often encountered when one attempts to get the patient to do anything else. Where the patient is perceptive and attentive to his own inner experiences, he becomes aware of a feeling of restlessness and of a desire to search after an indefinable "something." Intuition has guided doctors who often recommend a "cup of hot milk" to alleviate the insomnia.

The infant is the recipient of many varieties of stimuli arising from his environment including, of course, that which comes as a consequence of the physiological activity of his own body. And of all his sensory experiences it seems to me that those clustering about the nutritive functions are the more consistent and predictable. Every experience attendant upon or related to oral activity leaves its mark upon the psyche and contributes to shaping the developing ego. These stimuli, perhaps because of their universality and seeming triviality, have never been accorded the significance they deserve.

The earliest of life experiences—when the human clay is easily molded—influences the shape the character will take in adult life. The reader, of course, is already familiar with the basic tenet upon which the psychological sciences are built—namely, that one's present is the consequence of one's past experiences, especially those of childhood. Indeed, psychoanalysis is rather exclusively occupied with the responses of individuals to occurrences during childhood. The preverbal period of life, in contrast to later childhood, has received little attention, largely, one must suppose, because articulated memories do not exist. Content memories are not possible until there are verbal symbols with which to store them in the memory bank. In the practice of clinical psychiatry one finds that a variety of symptoms and even nonpathological phenomena can be most satisfactorily explained from knowledge of the details of the psychological mechanisms of the preverbal period of life. The details of preverbal psychic life will, because of their importance, be the principle object of our study.

Character molding begins within the context of the nursing experience. The interplay between the principals, mother and infant, has a profound and decisive effect upon the latter. The infant's perception of his own *Hunger Tide*, the response of the mother to the infant's signal cry of hunger, play their own important parts in the interpersonal transaction commonly referred to as "nursing." These are the principal ingredients between which there is a complexity of relationship having far-reaching effects on the configuration of the infant's character.

All of us begin the course we run in life within the compass of our mother's arms. And whether it be the biological mother or a de facto mother who nurses the infant, this fact alone has no logical significance for the child. One wonders, however, what the history of Rome would have been had Romulus and Remus been nursed by their own mother rather than by a wolf. Indeed, the feeding person can be male or female, for the concept of sexual difference has not yet dawned upon the infant and will not seem to him to be of any significance for several years to come. What is of first psychological significance to adults—the sex of another—is a matter of no discernible importance to the suckling.

This fact was impressed upon me years ago when, as an intern, I carried a newborn infant from the delivery room to the nursery. I held the child in my arms, and as I strode the corridor leading to the nursery I noted that the infant had gotten a fold of the surgical gown I was wearing into his mouth and was vigorously sucking on it! The infant was reacting reflexly. He was responding to a stimulus and the object of his reflex sucking was of no significance to him. It need not have been a piece of cloth. The object could as well have been a finger or a pacifier or a toy. Nor did the fact that it was a man who held him have any observable effect on his reflex response to oral impulses of biological origin. The one who held him and the object he sucked upon were outside the narrow limits of his comprehension. That both were biologically incapable of supplying milk had yet to be associated in his psyche. The object of the infant's sucking impulse has no psychological significance for him. That is precisely why, as I have supposed, there is no detectable difference in the psychological response of an infant to nursing a bottle or suckling at the breast.

The example I have given describing the manifestation of the sucking instinct in a newborn infant leaves unsolved the problem of the psychophysiological mechanism under whose aegis the reaction occurs. There is evidently an over-determination of the sucking behavior one observes in young infants. The mainsprings of the response seem to rest on multi-faceted gratifications which are obtained when the infant suckles. The apparent relish with which infants suck without relationship to nursing is evidence of a libidinal component whose significance and influence has yet to be fully assessed, not only during infancy but in adulthood as well.

The sucking of nonnutritive objects unquestionably provides libidinal gratification, derivatives of which continue through adult life. The search for libidinal oral gratification reenforces the physiological demands for nutriment. Undoubtedly this overdetermination of the sucking instinct is the product of long-term evolutionary processes common to the mammalia. Considering the absolute significance of incorporative behavior in terms of individual and species survival, one might, from this alone, surmise that there would be far-reaching psychological consequences relating thereto.

CHAPTER III

Suckling and Merging

Sucking is an instinct, the executive organs of which are well-developed and active prior to the time of birth. It has been well-documented, for example, that infants suck their thumbs in utero, and obviously the capacity to swallow is developed prior to birth. Early development of the capability to suck and swallow serves a vital survival function for the newborn. The sucking instinct is mediated through physiological reflex responses of oral executive structures to various stimulae. Later in life these reflexes undergo modification, just as do bladder and bowel reflexes. If the infant is touched on the cheek, this stimulus sets off a complex reflex in which the head is turned toward the side of the stimulus, the lips pursued, and sucking movements of the mouth initiated. Brushing a young anfant's lips with a finger tip evokes puckering and an attempt to suckle.

I have studied many aspects of the nursing situation and in the course of my endeavors I have made certain observations which have somehow, insofar as I have been able to learn, been entirely overlooked by earlier workers in the field. After I have defined them, the reader may confirm their existence by simply observing a small infant as he nurses. I have found it convenient to devise a terminology for these phenomena for which, until now, there have been no names. A complete list will be found in the Glossary of Terms at the end of the book.

For descriptive convenience I shall divide the phenomenon of suckling into three phases. Such divisions are, of course, arbitrary, but are employed because they facilitate the correlation of observed behavior with intrapsychic phenomena. The first phase is the preweaning period; the second is the *weaning period proper* (during which the *weaning process* is completed); and the third phase is the *postweaning period* (in which in all significant respects the child's manner of eating approximates the adult mode of alimentation).

Together the first two phases of suckling constitute the *weaning process,* a term with special meaning to be studied in detail subsequently. It is not possible to assign a precise number of weeks to the preweaning period of life, but generally speaking it extends from birth to about three months of age. There is no sharp line of demarcation between this and the subsequent weaning period proper, and perhaps it would serve as well to consider the entire period from birth until the adult mode of eating is established as the *weaning process.* There is similarly an overlapping of the *weaning period proper* and the *postweaning* period, for the *weaning process* is characterized by gradual shifts of "position" rather than by abrupt behavioral changes.

In the description of the phenomenon of suckling which follows, the reader must keep in mind that although the picture presented is accurate, there are subtle individual differences in the behavior of infants that cannot be readily detailed. I shall describe a model infant rather than one particular child.

We begin with the infant just beginning to cry in earnest because he perceives the pain of hunger pangs and, because of this, has just awakened from a period of sleep. The mother, hearing her infant cry, responds to his call. She goes to the infant, picks him up from the bed where he is lying, and holds him in her arm as she offers him her breast. The infant immediately stops his crying and takes the nipple into his mouth. Having grasped it with his lips he positions the nipple between tongue and hard palate. The jaw and tongue move rhythmically and the resultant suction produces a flow of milk. The milk, entering the oral pharynx, evokes the swallowing reflex and is delivered to the stomach, being carried there by the peristaltic movements of the esophagus. No sooner has the infant begun to suckle than his upper lids begin to droop until his eyes are partly or fully closed. His eyes rolls around in their sockets in an aimless sort of fashion which does not seem to follow, at least from gross observations, any particular pattern. These movements can be seen very clearly even though the eyes may be closed. The movements of the eyeball, readily observable in adults, are even more easily seen in infants. The impression of random and rapid eye movement is perhaps heightened because one cannot observe any relationship between the frequency of the eye movements and the rhythmic mandibular movements of sucking. Sometimes one observes divergence of the eyes as they move randomly in their sockets under closed lids. Dilatation of the peripheral blood vessels is a rather frequent concomitant of nursing. An infant's feet, for example, will appear pale and feel cold before he is nursed, and then become warm and pink as he suckles. The entire skin participates in this vasodilator response, but is is especially noticeable in the flush area. Of course, in the dark-skinned only the temperature changes noted above can be observed. Very frequently a mild diaphorsesis accompanies the vasodilatation, more readily observable in warm weather than in cold. The evacuation of urine and feces is sometimes an accompaniment of suckling, but I do not know if there is a consistent or meaningful relationship between the two.

In addition to these physiological phenomena, there is still another observation which, because of its psychological importance, has been left for last so that it can be considered in relationship to the physiological responses just described. Though more difficult to describe in precise and specific terminology, there is no doubt that "something" happens within the infant as he suckles during the *preweaning period* which does not happen at all when he takes nourishment during the postweaning period! An alteration of a quite specific psychological nature envelops the infant each time he suckles during the *preweaning period*. This psychological phenomenon has been variously described by those I have questioned. Some of the expressions employed to describe the phenomenon are recorded to give the reader a feel for what transpires within the infant. The following are responses to requests for descriptions of what seems to occur to a young infant as he suckles: "The infant is enjoying complete abandonment —not a care in the world"; "Everything is rosy"; "It's ecstasy for the child"; "He's out of this world"; "He's on 'cloud nine'"; "He just isn't with you any more"; and "He's lost to everything now." One especially verbal woman told me, when I asked her to describe for me as best she could what she believed her infant girl was experiencing after she had begun nursing. "She was gone way out—I have often thought when I observed this that this was what it should be like in sexual intercourse." I have interviewed some mothers who could not recall ever having seen the response I have described. But then some people are unobservant by nature. The consensus has been, and my personal observations confirm, that such responses not only are "real" but are invariably displayed during infancy.

I shall trace the course followed by this particular phenomenon from birth until the time it no longer occurs. The libidinal quality of the infant's psychological response to nursing is clearly reflected in the descriptive phrases I have just quoted. Indeed, the infant does seem to "dissolve," to employ a term suggested by one mother. I have chosen the word *"to merge"* to describe this phenomenon because, to my way of thinking, it comes closest to articulating what the infant experiences when he suckles. There is no word in the English language that defines the specifiic event for which I employ the term *"merging."* When an infant nurses he becomes "one" with the mother, figuratively *merging* with her. The physical union is accompanied by a psychological union of the most intense sort.

When we consider the descriptions others have supplied of this phenomenon of *merging* and add to them the data obtained from a considerable amount of personal observation, there can be no question that the infant undergoes a libidinal experience uniquely and exclusively associated with suckling. It will be noted that each of the foregoing observations were interpretations of the events rather than precise descriptions thereof. *Merging* was described by analogy for the simple reason that no other framework suffices. The uniformity of these descriptions in terms of of the idea of psychic change they convey is, to my way of thinking, quite impressive. It strongly suggests that the idea of a shift of psychological position while nursing is valid. The implications of this response for subsequent psychological development must be approached tangentially. One needs almost to devise a technique for the purpose. The contrast between the infant's capability of relating to objects outside himself with his utter abandonment of outside objects as he *merges* during the act of suckling becomes ever more striking with the passage of time. At about the age of a month until the age of about three months one observes the emergence of a primitive ego which, as maturation proceeds, becomes progressively more clearly defined. The *weaning period* proper has its beginnings during this time of early ego differentiation. It is the *weaning process* which is the principal subject of of interest. This term has been chosen to indicate that the weaning of an infant is a complex, time-consuming process rather than a parent-determined change of diet. Just prior to the *weaning process* the infant merged each time he suckled, unaware of having undergone the experience of "losing" himself. The ego mechanism by which the awareness of *merging* can be realized coincides in its development with the commencement of the *weaning process*. By about the third month of life the ego has developed sufficient awareness of itself to recognize the form, if not the content, of experiences which influence its own judging

41

and evaluating functions. In my judgment the smiling response is an observable indicator of the fact that this has been achieved.

The *merging*, which up to the initiation of the *weaning process* had no meaning or particular significance to the infant, begins to confront an ego which increasingly appreciates its own expanding capacity to mediate between the demands from various sources made upon it. The infant now comes to perceive what before had gone unnoticed, namely, that when he *merges*, during the act of suckling, his ego boundaries crumble and cease to exist. Examining the situation from the infant's viewpoint one can well imagine that it appears to him that each time he *merges* he ceases to exist. But the *merging* is not renounced on account of this impression. There is no intellect yet present to deal with what I believe to be an increasing concern with an unavoidable anxiety-producing circumstance. Each time the infant nurses he *merges*, and in so doing his barely established ego boundaries dissolve.

The mother who remarked that when her infant nursed it appeared to her that he was "no longer with it" put the matter in frank idiomatic terms. What she meant was that the infant no longer related to her during the nursing act in the same way that he had prior to or after being fed. This, the reader will observe, is the implication of all the interpretive descriptions quoted earlier. It was my own impression, when observing the *merging* phenomenon in infants, that the child vacated whatever relationship he had established with an object outside himself during the act of nursing and was, moreover, quite incapable of doing otherwise. For this phenomenon of *merging*, not one of choice for the nursling, is not a sometime thing. It is an omnipresent and obligate reaction which is part and parcel of the complex act of sucking. The extensive implications of the *merging response* will be dealt with in a later chapter. Before exploring it further, however, I shall describe and give a name to another phenomenon observable in nursing infants.

The *quiver response* is the term I employ to designate a phenomenon that is sometimes observable toward the termination of nursing sessions. While it is an event which occurs inconsistently, it is my impression that it is experienced by every infant. Whether or not it is an invariant occurrence during the infantile period remains to be determined. The infant's body "stiffens up" for a few moments, following which his entire body becomes involved in a species of rhythmic shaking. The entire reaction runs its course in about five seconds. In more technical terms, the infant, when he undergoes a *quiver response*, develops a generalized tonic muscular contraction (where the extensors dominate over the flexors) which, without interval, is followed by a short series of generalized clonic contractions. The reaction commences and terminates without arousing the infant from the *merging* which was present at its inception. Suckling ceases and is not renewed once the *quiver response* begins. As far as I can determine, the *quiver response* never occurs save from a "position" of *merging*, and at the very end of a feeding. Indeed, it can be interpreted, I think, as an especially intense occasion of *merging*. Alternatively, it may represent the *merging response* carried to its ultimate physical and psychological expression.

It is no easy matter to confirm the existence of the *quiver response* by personal observation. It requires a good deal of patience which is apt to be rewarded at the very time one's interest and attention lags. Nonetheless, confirmation is obtainable not only from mothers but also from the nurses and attendants who care for nurslings in a hospital setting. Of course, as with the *merging response*, whether or not the observation is made depends upon the perceptiveness of the observer. The vast majority of those I have queried confirm the presence of the "*quiver response.*" A few have denied ever witnessing such a reaction in any of their charges. Neither this phenomenon nor the *merging response* seem to have drawn any special attention or curiosity. Both have been considered, by those I have questioned, as natural, normal events during infancy. Several nurses showed surprise that a physician would have any interest in what they considered unremarkable, everyday occurrences. The general familiarity of observant women who work in hospital nursery settings with the *quiver response* gives virtual assurance that it is a normal part of infantile experience.

People in general reserve the question "Why?" for the extraordinary. The scientific "position," in contrast, demands to know the "why" of every event. Nothing is "too insignificant," "too commonplace," or "too trivial" to justify intensive, serious study; the basic premise being that no phenomenon can be overlooked or disregarded if knowledge is to expand. I shall return to an examination of the *quiver response* in a subsequent chapter when the way has been further prepared for a discussion of the implications of this physiological reaction in infancy.

In summary then, we have observed how the infant *merges* as he suckles and thus "loses" whatever individual identity he has achieved at this point in his development. A *quiver response* involving a general increase in muscular tonus and a few seconds of clonic movements sometimes is observable as a terminal event of a nursing session. Following this, the infant drifts into a state of sleep.

From the ontological point of view there can be no question as to the survival significance of the oral instinct. It is the first instinct to make its appearance in the developing fetus, and it survives even though the higher cerebral centers be malformed or partly destroyed by disease or injury. I once observed an 88-year-old man in a hospital suffering from a severe organic brain syndrome. So impaired was his cerebral functioning that he was incapable of relating in any way with those around him. Yet despite

the ovewhelming severity of the disease process he ceaselessly and repetitiously moaned "mama, mama," until at
last death took him.

The capacity to suck develops in utero, but at what
stage of embryological development is not known precisely. The quantity of instinctual drive appears to be in
excess of that required to assure the newborn will suckle
and thus survive. The overabundant sucking impulse seeks
discharge for that excess quantity not discharged in the act
of nursing. Nonnutritive sucking behavior, by reducing
physiological tensions, serves to alleviate discomfort resulting from the damming up of instinctual energy. The
sucking impulse seems incapable of satiation through food
intake alone. Indeed, throughout life oral activity or the
psychological derivatives thereof unconnected with nutrition, seems universal.

The pleasure or libidinal component of sucking behavior
is what gives it the stamp of an instinct. The same idea can
be expressed from another point of view by conceiving of
the pleasure aspect of sucking as a reinforcement of the
physiologically determined sucking instinct. It seems quite
certain that the infant "gets something" or derives gratification from sucking his thumb. Indeed, one could not
imagine what might motivate such behavior were it otherwise. Thumb sucking undoubtedly supplies a different sort
of pleasure than sucking an object not anatomically part
of the infant. For with thumb sucking there is the experience of sensations arising both from the mouth which
performs the sucking, and the thumb which is being
sucked. When the infant has for his object something
other then a part of his own anatomy, sensory impulses
flow to the infant's central nervous system from his mouth
alone. How these differences between pacifier sucking and
thumb sucking may influence the developing ego is not
presently known. Nor has sufficient attention been accorded
the questions that arise when breast feeding is compared
with bottle feeding. I have observed infants *merge* while

sucking a pacifier, so one may conclude from this that *merging* is related to the sucking instinct itself rather than to the object of the instinct. I have never personally seen the *quiver response* occur except when an infant is nursing.

Immediately after birth there is little discernible change in the appearance the infant presents when he nurses. That is to say, the ego-less state already exists before nursing commences. The fact of *merging* becomes increasingly evident because this state contrasts so sharply with the infant's increasing relatedness to those around him. As the preweaning period tapers off, insensibly shifting to the *weaning period proper,* the contrasts between the infant's psychic status before, during, and after suckling become truly impressive. As he matures he shows responsiveness of growing complexity in regard to objects outside himself. But every time he nurses the infant relinquishes all object relationship and *merges* as he has since birth.

The intrapsychic activity of the infant as he nurses must remain forever a matter of conjecture and circumstantial evidence. As far as one can tell, there is affect but not content. It is no simple or certain task to translate the events experienced within the experiential universe of the infant into an intellectually comprehensible idiom. To understand the influence of various factors encountered during the preverbal period of life upon the psyche requires considering events "as though" the infant has certain powers of conceptualization. Analogy is a limited but valued tool, and perhaps the only one employable under the circumstances. There are very great limitations imposed by such a necessity, limitations with which the reader has already had experience if he is at all familiar with writings which popularize science. Complex concepts of a mathematical nature, for example, are converted to analogy so that the nonmathematician may at least get a glimpse of concepts unsuited to the language and ideas of "common sense." For the present there seems little hope of improving on the technique because the experience of *merging* cannot, for obvious reasons, be reported upon directly by the infant, nor can such reactions be remembered in the usual sense that things are remembered with recallable words. Later, when I discuss the entire history of the *merging response* and its implications for psychology, the reader will perhaps get a more convincing feel for it. Of course, most convincing of all would be the actual observation of nursing infants. The concept of the *merging* and *quiver responses* are of more than academic interest. There is an abundance of clinical material, both normal and pathological, that can now be satisfactorily explained in relationship to the *merging response.*

CHAPTER IV

The Weaning Process

It is curious that the *merging response,* which appears to be an integral part of the sucking instinct, has not been delineated by students of early infantile life. Since older children and adults do not *merge* when they eat, it is evident that the *merging response* changes and disappears. As I have indicated, the merging response does not disappear all at once, but undergoes progressive modification until it succumbs to the repressive forces of the developing ego. It is also evident that "something psychological" happens within the infant to cause him to relinquish the obvious libidinal gratifications of *merging,* as well as the satisfactions of the occasional tremor response he experiences at the end of a nursing session. We have no hope whatever of being told by an infant what he experiences, nor is it possible for him to "remember" in later life and communicate with words what he felt as an infant. There is no technique available to the infant by which information can be coded and stored in the memory bank for subsequent ideational retrieval. Not until the ego begins to develop as a distinct entity do the first glimmerings of associations of time-related events occur within the psyche in verbally reproducible form.

The precursor of the capacity to reason is discoverable in the early primitive logical devices of time-related and space-related association. Adults suffering from schizophrenia and even from other less enveloping degrees of immaturity invariably rely heavily upon such primitive techniques of reasoning. It is for just such reason that therapeutic efforts fail so often to accomplish their objectives. These unfortunates never advance psychologically beyond the infantile theory that two events simultaneous, or nearly so, in space or time must by virtue thereof have an etiological relationship one with the other. Presumably, at one time in the history of mankind such "reasoning" served a useful survival function. Immature people, however diagnostically classified, characteristically feel, think and act in concrete terms. In view of the afore-mentioned absence of verbal memories of transactions during early life, we must, if we are to be enlightened, employ an investigative technique different from that found so useful in the analysis of psychic phenomena arising subsequent to the acquisition of language.

In the same manner that the anthropologist reconstructs for us the probable appearance of primitive man and speculates on the circumstances in which he lived, with no more evidence than a few bone fragments and artifacts, I shall attempt to reconstruct the psychological reactions of the infant to weaning from the available data.

The first source of data is the capacity of people to "empathize." The *merging response,* for example, could not have been defined from the psychological side had the subjective impressions of observers been discounted. When different observers repeatedly arrive at impressions quite similar in content, then more than casual significance can be accorded this evidence. Especially so, I believe, in the observations made on *merging,* because not one person suggested that such a phenomenon, however described, was not a palpable reality. The second source of data is the field of clinical medicine. The third is derived from analysis of the behavior, attitude and fantasy of adults—patients with whom detailed investigation has been conducted. When this data is subjected to inductive reasoning and the conclusions allow no reasonable alternative formulation, then one has reasonable assurance that his theory is valid. This impression is strengthened, moreover, when from the details of a patient's character and symptoms one can prepare a character sketch of the mother (without, of course, prior knowledge), to the accuracy of which the patient attests. On occasion when one learns of a women's behavior with her grandchildren, the supporting data derived therefrom is quite convincing. The repetition compulsion ensures that a mother will behave toward her infant grandchildren as she once did toward her own children. If, for example, she disregards a grandchild's need for milk and feeds him as she decides he requires, one may be certain that she is replaying an old attitude.

The sucking reflex becomes conditioned and modified as the infant matures. For example, we know that in response to being held in the nursing position the nursling will turn its head in the direction of the breast. This response of the infant seems to operate without the participation of conscious discriminative awareness of the infant's spacial relationship with a source of food. One can show, for example, that the young infant will turn his mouth away from the chest of the person holding him if the nipple of the bottle or even a finger touches his cheek on the off side. He will, moreover, nurse in that position as easily as in the more usual posture. One rather fastidious nurse I observed always fed the infant in her charge in just such a position, explaining that "if they should have an accident (emesis) it won't get all over my uniform." This somewhat awkward position seemed, so far as could be observed, to make no difference to the infant, who suckled and *merged* as well when held this way as in any other manner. As the infant matures the reflex is superseded by discriminative behavior which takes precedence; he follows the logic of association and turns to the presenting breast or bottle unhesitatingly, being guided now by his eye more than by automatic reflexes.

But over and beyond these maturational advances there are parallel psychological events of the greatest importance taking place. The infant's ego is developing. From the state of non-ego—that is, a state of undifferentiation in which he has no awareness of himself as distinct and apart from the world around him—the infant comes to an awareness that continues to expand the boundaries through recognition of which he acquires the capability of separating self from non-self. At first the ego boundaries are tenuous and uncertainly defined. One can observe this fact in operation when an infant "discovers" some part of his anatomy with which he has had, up to this time, no meaningful confrontation. When, for example, he "discovers" his toes, most adults react with amusement and intuitively understand that the infant is puzzled and cannot grasp a fact which has been, to the adult, self-evident for many years. Discovering a part of one's self is a different category of experience than, say, discovering a rattle or a toy. For in the former the object explored by the hand also registers sensation as a consequence of that exploration. There is the simultaneous perception of feeling the size, shape and texture of an object via the hand, and the sensation the manipulations of the exploring hand exercises on the toes. Sensory stimuli flow centripedally from both sources. In contrast, an object not an anatomical feature of the infant is clearly outside himself, since a stimulus is relayed to the central nervous system by the exploring portion of the anatomy alone.

At the very beginning of the differentiation process the ego boundaries, not yet being firmly established, are frequently relinquished. This dissolution of ego boundaries is what occurs, from the psychological side, each time the infant *merges*. Only gradually does he come to place value on that state of awareness which *is* the ego. The infant becomes increasingly aware of himself through his perceptive apparatus, which has all along been completing its anatomical development and becoming to an increasing degree physiologically mature and functional. Without a sensory apparatus no ego at all could evolve. As the infant becomes increasingly aware of his sensory perceptions, as more and more he correctly categorizes and differentiates sensory experiences as different from one another as seeing, hearing, smelling, tasting, and feeling, he gradually comes to the recognition that his increasingly valued ego relinquishes its perceptive capacity each time he nurses. Each time he nurses he *merges;* behavior which is regressive in terms of his developing capacity to relate to objects. It seems likely that he continues to *merge,* because of the gratifying libidinal quality of the experience. Like all "habits" the pleasure received through its performance maintains it. At the same time that the infant becomes aware of the pleasure of *merging,* he comes to recognize that during the period of time he experiences this gratification, increasingly valued perceptive capacities of his ego cease to exist. One cannot "lose oneself" during *merging* and, at the same time, maintain object relationships. Something has to give! A clear-cut choice seems to be presented by the contending forces. Either the *merging* is to be retained, *or* the integrity of the ego is to be protected! The issue is not settled all at once, but rather is dealt with by a series of compromises, themselves reflected in observable behavior as the forces of anatomical, physiological and psychological maturation press relentlessly onward.

This confrontation of incompatible aims occurs between two and half and three months of age when the infant finds himself in the impossible situation of wishing to lose his ego and keep it too! Because of an overriding ascendancy of the ego, each time the infant suckles, the attendant *merging* is increasingly perceived as an annihilatory event. A compromise is sought within which it first seems that the perceptive capacities of the ego *and* the sensual pleasures of *merging* have achieved a workable balance acceptable to the ego. The *merging,* earlier invariably present when the infant suckled, gradually becomes relegated to the final portion of each feeding. It does not, however, simply disappear. Replacing it is a phenomenon which has received considerable attention, despite which, curiously enough, its description has not given heed to what in my judgment are its most outstanding and characteristic features—features which specifically set it apart from similar behavior and with which it has been misidentified.

As *merging* is gradually relinquished the infant may be observed to gaze at the mother's face as it suckles for progressively longer portions of each feeding. This gaze is so unique, so easily distinguishable from all other kinds of looking, that I find it appropriate and useful to give it a special designation. *Raptus* is the unswerving, unblinking, wide-eyed, hypnotic, transfixed, focusless gaze which replaces *merging* as the infant suckles. Unlike other varieties of looking, the gaze is steady and imperturbable; even passing a hand across the infant's line of vision fails to gain his attention in contrast to other times when almost any movement within the compass of his sight distracts him. Whereas the *merging* reaction was accompanied by aimless conjugate wandering of the eye beneath partly or wholly closed lids, in *raptus* the eyes are fixed and unblinking. Nor do they reflect the comprehension with which, on other occasions, the infant observes events about him. I interpret *raptus* as the compromise by which an infant attempts to deal with the paradox defined earlier. In *raptus* the ego neither dissolves nor entirely retains its boundaries. For a time, at least, this compromise is acceptable to the ego. The proportion of time spent in *raptus* increases as it gradually replaces *merging*, a movement necessitated by an ego increasingly intolerant of the loss it experiences when *merging*. It is against the backdrop of progressive anatomical development and unremitting physiological activity that the vicissitudes of the suckling reflex must be studied to be appreciated.

The reader will appreciate the technical problem of presenting an accurate comprehensive description of the sequential behavior which, taken altogether, I designate the *weaning process;* the same difficulty would be encountered if one wished to describe a movie but, lacking a projector, was required to describe it frame by frame. It would soon be found that noting the differences between every 25th frame would prove much more informative than considering each one in sequence. Thus, in describing the *weaning process* I present as discrete occurrences what is actually a smooth progression of one phenomenon, first blending with and then supplanting its predecessor. There is an observable transition from the response of *merging*, which from birth until the commencement of the *weaning process* coincides in time with the duration of each nursing session to *merging* not observable until the last few moments of suckling. An inverse relationship between *merging* and the *raptus* which replaces it is readily demonstrable. As the former decreases, more time is devoted to the latter. *Raptus,* in turn, is gradually supplanted. A progressive inverse relationship develops between it and a developing relatedness to objects outside itself even as the infant suckles. When at last *raptus* is displaced by the focused, attentive looking and perceptiveness that characterizes the mealtime attitude of adults, the *weaning process* has been completed and the *adult mode* of eating has been achieved. Weaning is the process by which the supremacy of the ego is established over the forces of the oral instinct.

I am aware that this definition is not the conventional one. To wean, in the ordinary sense, it to cause a child to become accustomed to food other than its mother's milk—to stop suckling. This definition, however, has a serious drawback. It defines the word "weaning" by emphasizing the substitution of one form of nutrient for another. By this definition a person who continued to drink milk all his life would never be weaned! And this is clearly not the idea conveyed by the word "weaning." Even the idea that weaning means a cessation of sucking is not an adequate definition. For there are cultures in which older children continue to suckle occasionally and, as in the preceding example, cannot be considered "unweaned." The customary meaning is more plainly put, of course, by saying that weaning occurs when one is taken off the breast or bottle. But the matter is not so simple. Let us consider it further.

What happens, for example, if an infant is not "taken off the breast"? The dictionary has it that weaning is accomplished through an action of the mother. It is she who substitutes one food for another. Does that mean that if for some reason the mother did not remove the bottle or breast, the individual would never relinquish suckling as a way of obtaining food? The answer is more easily given than explained. Certainly more is involved than withdrawal of breast or bottle. Mothers will tell you that there comes a time when a child will refuse or reject breast or bottle even if it offered when he is obviously hungry. We recognize that the dictionary definition is not sufficient for our purposes because it disregards the psychological aspects of the process.

Human weaning is a psychophysiological phenomenon most usefully described as a process, one of the indices of whose completion is the attainment of an *adult mode* of consuming food and drink. The process evolves over a period of time and is subject to many influences, some of which are decisive in determining the characteristics of the adult ego. I think it is evident that the shift from an *infantile mode* to an adult mode of response while taking nourishment represents a psychophysiological advance of considerable complexity. The nature of the nutrient itself is of relative insignificance compared to the total psychophysiological involvement in the *weaning process*. It is, therefore, the slow evolution of a psychological process leading from the infantile to the *adult mode* of alimentation that constitutes weaning in the sense that it will be used henceforth.

I have already discussed the *infantile mode* without, however labeling it as such. The reader will recall that during the early weeks after birth the infant regularly *merges* as he nurses and occasionally displays a quiver *response* as well. There is a gradual replacement of the *merging response* by *raptus*. This phase of the weaning process represents the *infantile mode* and certainly deserves to be so distinguished from the *adult mode* of eating; the manifest differences are striking and specific. The *adult mode* is followed by older children and adults. Here, neither *merging* nor *raptus* is observed and—of the greatest significance—the ego keeps as much in perceptual contract with its surroundings when a person eats as at other waking moments. Most of us enjoy eating in the company of others simultaneously socializing as we chew and swallow and use our eating implements. Adults, in contrast to young infants pursue other interests as they eat. Indeed, the idea of a healthy *merging* as he eats is inconceivable. The transformations which are brought about through the *meaning process* usually proceed in an orderly manner. We next turn to the details of the transition from the *infantile mode* to the *adult mode* of ego conduct.

The transition is subject to many vicissitudes, the consequences of which have far-reaching effects upon the psyche. We have learned that growth of the infant's ego is attested to by an expanding capacity to perceive circumstances which earlier in his development had no meaning for him. The infant, becoming aware of the *merging* experience, responds to it in a specific way. As a result of this response the *merging* response is progressively modified to *raptus* which ultimately entirely displaces it. The compromise between *merging* and the maintenance of outside object relationships which, psychologically considered, *raptus* represents, does not for long satisfy the requirements of an ego progressively extending its boundaries. The time comes when the infant is confronted by a second dilemma similar to that encountered when to *merge* or not to *merge* became the question: Shall the ego maintain its full perceptive awareness during a nursing session, or shall a state of *raptus* continue to accompany suckling?

The conflict engendered by the *weaning paradox* has as

many solutions as there are individuals. And it seems not unlikely that a close relationship exists between the precise details of the solution and the uniqueness of form the personality ultimately assumes. The infant may, for example, refuse the breast but take the bottle, or accept spooned food and reject both breast and bottle. And he may do this for one or two feedings and then be willing to accept what he had previously rejected. A period of trial "solutions" which varies in duration from a few days to months is readily observable.

We must pause at the threshold of this dilemma, put off our discussion for a moment, and remind ourselves that all the while anatomical maturation has been on the march. Of considerable significance is the eruption of teeth beginning at about the sixth month, introducing a new circumstance into the *weaning process*. The lower incisors appear at about this time. As a consequence physiological reactions of some complexity are set into motion. The gums overlying the erupting teeth become edematous and hyperemic. Salivation increases, possibly as a consequence of this tissue reaction, and a slight fever is very frequently observed. That many infants experience discomfort and pain when they teethe appears quite certain. It seems reasonable to suppose that infants "discover" that a slight pressure upon the inflamed gingiva overlying the lower incisors will produce relief from discomfort. When bitten gently the edema is reduced, the tension in the gingival tissue accordingly is lessened and the pain is ameliorated. But if an infant bites "hard"—if he closes his jaws so that the pressure upon the gingiva exceeds a critical limit—the pain, instead of being relieved, becomes more intense. This is due to the fact that the gingiva is traumatized by being forced against the sharp edges of the erupting teeth. It must be most difficult for an infant to "understand" how biting which has produced no remarkable conscious sensation suddenly has the capability of producing both relief *and* pain. What the meaning of this event has for the infant depends not only upon his chronological age, but the maturational status of the ego at that time as well. It can, of course, be meaningless if it occurs before the ego has made much progress in its development, or it can form the basis for an "infantile theory" by reference to which subsequent behavior is related until such time as this particular "theory" is replaced by one more relevant.

For the first time since birth the infant now is confronted with the factor of degree. Prior to teething the child has reckoned existence as an all-or-nothing affair. But now, by virtue of the teething experience, the concept of quantity is introduced. In the infant's frame of reference it must appear that a gentle bite is "good" or gratifying and a hard bite is "bad" or painful. Moreover, if the infant is being breast fed, his biting will prove painful to the mother and produce a response of some kind from her. When, in contrast, the infant is bottle fed, it seems likely that any the association established in the infant's mind between "biting" and withdrawal of the source of milk will not be so clear-cut.

As the infant matures physically and psychologically, the *merging* response when suckling gives way after two or three months to *raptus* as he suckles. The appearance of *raptus* reflects the operation of the process whereby the *infantile mode* of behavior is transformed into the *adult mode*. The *merging response* has been modified by the growing ego of the infant. A compromise—the assumption of a psychological position between the alert attentiveness of the waking state and the withdrawal of the *merging response*—is achieved.

This compromise is the first of a series of "solutions" which follow one after the other concomitant with maturation of the ego. There are two contending aims vying for gratification. One is the instinctual libidinal gratification experienced during suckling and *merging,* while a contending aim has arisen as a characteristic of the developing ego itself. It is through the latter that the gratifications of re-

58

ality are progressively conceived as superior to the libidinal gratification of suckling. The enigma that arises in relationship to these two aims drives the *weaning process* to its ultimate conclusion—the assumption of the *adult mode* of taking nourishment and its correlary, adult behavior of all kinds. On the one hand the infant is tempted to indulge his accustomed libidinal gratification of relinquishing reality as food is taken in, while on the other there is an intensification of the fear of *merging*—an experience increasingly apprehended by the maturing ego as threatening. Later in this work we will see how this burgeoning awareness relates to the "fear of death" and "fear of insanity"—commonplace symptoms both in and out of clinical psychiatric practice.

One can observe that, with the passage of time, the evolving fixed and vacant gaze of the nursing infant progresses less and less frequently to *merging*—behavior invariably encountered in the early phases of the *weaning process*. It can also be observed that *raptus* itself gradually changes in character until ultimately a psychological position of adult attentiveness to matters outside and entirely unrelated to the intake of food is assumed. The harbinger of the *adult mode* is recognized when, during a nursing session, the infant begins to look at objects attentively. A noise, a door slamming for example, may distract him from his suckling once the adult mode has made its appearance, whereas during *merging* and *raptus* disturbances of this nature have little if any affect upon the infant's nursing. Once the *adult mode* has begun to displace *raptus* the infant will stop nursing and attend to such stimuli, seeking its source with his eyes. Moreover, the infant will respond to the mother, even relinquishing the nipple to return her smile. And when the infant no longer *merges* at all—when he eats without the fixed, hypnotic gaze of *raptus* and is able to take in nourishment and at the same time relate to objects outside himself—the end of the *weaning process* has been achieved and the infant

59

henceforth eats according to the *adult mode*.

But why, as has been declared, should the infant fear *merging?* How could an experience with which he is so familiar and which, moreover, is unquestionably gratifying, arouse the emotion of fear? The infant comes to fear *merging* because during the time of this experience he vacates his ego. It must be recalled that the infant has an extremely limited "tunnel vision" view of life. He has no time sense, nor does he yet possess language. He is abysmally ignorant of reality and his "universe" extends no further than the compass of his mother's arms. At first he does not even appreciate that he himself is an entity, distinct, unique, and different from all other objects. His ego develops out of the id, the primeval mud, as it were. Once it is recognized as apart from, rather than a part of, the objects about him, the ego achieves a position of paramount importance. It is at once the core of one's own uniqueness and a means by which its own boundaries are extended. It becomes the infant's most precious possession. The ego develops to the point where each time the infant *merges* he senses that somehow the previously tenuous boundaries of his universe dissolve as he suckles and he no longer exists as a recognizable entity. The clinical signs of this psychological phenomenon may be followed by observing how *merging* progresses through *raptus* to the *adult mode*. The experience is probably akin to that anxiety experienced by some when submitting to general anesthesia. The same sort of fear response may be involved in persons who resist hypnosis.

At the early time of life when the *weaning process* has just commenced, the infant has no conscious control over *merging*. It is, as far as I can tell, obligatory. But as the ego capacities increase he becomes capable of modifying the *merging response* for increasingly longer periods of each nursing session. This modification, or *raptus,* is distinguished by characteristic ocular manifestations. The state of *raptus* is not so profoundly "out of it," nor does

60

it remove the infant so far from reality as *merging*. It is out of the fear of *merging* that the infant finds the compromise reaction of *raptus* (the fear of *merging* has far-reaching consequences, to be considered subsequently). *Raptus* itself is relinquished when it in turn becomes no longer acceptable to an increasingly astute ego, jealous of its own integrity. And when *raptus* phases out of the picture the *weaning process* is completed; the *adult mode* of eating is established once the infant has successfully eliminated, through repression, the primitive libidinal aspects of eating.

But, one may ask, isn't sleeping also a loss of ego? And isn't it, in fact, identical with *merging?* And if there is a fear of *merging* as claimed, why doesn't the infant fear sleep?

One can certainly agree that sleep is a manifestation of withdrawal of ego contact with the outside world. But beyond this the similarity of sleep with *merging* seems more apparent than real. For sleep comes to the infant in response to fatigue and is under the control of demonstrable sleeping and waking centers in the brain. We do not know of a central nervous system center for the *merging response*. Nor is sleep characterized by the constant, random movements of the eyes observable in the *merged* infant. Moreover, infantile *merging* occurs only in relationship to suckling and at no other time. It occurs at a time when, were it not for the involvement in obtaining nutrition, the infant would be fully awake and alert to his surroundings. An adult gradually relinquishes his contact with external reality and goes to sleep because of fatigue. Indeed, if he is not tired he cannot do so. It seems quite probable that some instances of insomnia—and especially that sleeplessness regularly accompanying depressive reactions—are due to psychopathological associations where sleep is equated with a longed-for but dangerous and forbidden *merging*. General anesthesia is frequently feared because the latter offers to deprive an individual of his contact with the world at a moment when he is very much alert and aware. The "fear" is momentary, but nonetheless very real, and many people who have undergone the experience of general anesthesia can testify to this fact—if they are asked about it before experience undergoes repression. Of course, some individuals develop a comforting amnesia and will deny any such reaction. But for most people a loss of consciousness—or even the idea of such—is felt as threatening. Sleep is not a loss of consciousness, but rather a withdrawal of contact with external reality.

All along I have used the model of an infant at breast or bottle in discussing the *weaning process*. I need only add that the same process is normally carried to the achievement of the *adult mode* of eating regardless of the technique of feeding followed by the mother. I have seen infants *merge* when spoon fed and I have observed *raptus* many times as a nurse tried to spoon food into an infant's mouth. Though the child does not think in words or concepts in the manner of adults, I consider that from his naive and limited point of view the situation shapes up something like this: "If I suckle I *merge* and lose my identity. If I don't suckle I don't lose myself but I pay for it by having hunger pangs." And even though it be determined not to *merge* and to accomplish this by not suckling, such a "solution" is obviously self-defeating and cannot be long maintained. An insoluble paradox? No. Indeed, as we have now learned, the curious open-eyed ocular fixation—*raptus*—serves admirably as a compromise solution. Some of the libidinal elements of *merging* are given up, in exchange for which the ego is not entirely submerged.

There are uncounted "solutions" to the weaning paradox, differing from each other not in kind but in quality and extent of compromise. There are unique subtleties in the *weaning process* of each individual, the transition from *infantile mode* to *adult mode* being carried on with varying degrees of success. I say "varying degrees of success" for I think absolute and complete renunciation of infantile wishes to be unattainable. Sometimes the *weaning process* is so unsuccessfully concluded that the ego's future development is permanently compromised. There is an infinite variety of "incompletenesses" of the *weaning process,* and the psychopathological consequences of these are to be considered in some detail. So far I have concentrated on the details of the vicissitudes of the sucking impulse during infancy, but now I shall present examples of infantile behavior reflecting the search for solutions to the *weaning paradox.*

A friend of mine has a child who did what many infants do—he signaled his readiness to relinquish his bottle by pulling out the rubber nipple with his teeth while it was still full of milk. Quite a mess was created, of course. "Formula" was spilled all over the crib and the child, on the rug, and a few stray drops even found their way to an adjacent wall. And, just as other parents have described this kind of "inexplicable" behavior with amused tolerance implicit in the tone of their voices, so did my friend. Why did he become amused, and why was there a tinge of pride as he related this story? Why wasn't he angry at the trouble his child's behavior had caused? I think he unconsciously recognized that such behavior was a step in the direction of maturity. This is the manner in which most parents deal with this kind of event. Far from being critical or punitive, they encourage such displays of "independence."

Another child hurled his bottle from his crib almost across the room, smashing it and putting his parents on notice that he was on the verge of making decisions to eat after the manner of adults. He was announcing with as much emphasis as he could muster that he was relinquishing the libidinal component of eating.

Another infant found her particular and unique solution to the *weaning paradox.* She had been breast fed for three months, after which she had been bottle fed. At the end of nine months—so her mother related, a little angrily (but with a tone of amusement and pride in her voice)—"You know what that little stinker of mine did? The other day she took her bottle—it's a plastic one, you know—and she turned it upside down and just squeezed the milk all over the place. Then this morning she did the same thing. Can you imagine? Four ounces of milk all over her crib and the floor and all over everything! I said to her, 'O.K., kid, that's it, that's all for you! From now on you get it in a cup.' And I mean it, doctor—she's just trying to tell me and I understand, believe me, I really understand!" One observes that here too the infant is giving notice that she no longer wishes to suckle her food according to the *infantile mode*.

Why does she give up the bottle? The evidence is not clear-cut, but I think there is enough to justify an interpretation. The infant seeks a solution to a paradox. She is attempting to control matters. She is trying to master the nursing situation during which she earlier *merged* and thereby "lost" her unique and presently highly valued identity. Her apparent disdain for the milk suggests that her trial-and-error solution to the paradox is to avoid *merging* through the renunciation of suckling. Note how accurately the mother assesses the situation. Henceforth she will feed her daughter by cup, and in so doing will join forces with her in the baby's search for domination of the ego over the oral instinctual impulses.

There follows another solution to the weaning paradox, one which is self-defeating but which, nonetheless, is one that infants often try in their efforts to achieve an anxiety-free compromise. The infant may refuse to suckle! Undoubtedly this course would be persisted in were it not for the increasingly imperative demands of the hunger pangs. So the infant is forced to abandon this tentative solution and seek one in which the *weaning paradox* can be solved in a way consistent with survival. Such "experiments" on the infant's part are often observable. The most impressive example I have witnessed occurred with the infant of a neighbor.

The mother had picked up her 6½ month-old daughter because the child had begun to cry and was obviously hungry. She had heated a bottle and, holding the child in her arms, offered her the nipple. The child squirmed and made it very evident that she did not want to suckle. The mother took the bottle from the infant's view and she quieted down. Once more she offered it and again the child "fought" the nipple. So the mother placed the infant in its nearby crib and propped the bottle on a pillow. Without the slightest hesitation the infant pulled the nipple to its mouth and began to suckle!

This whole affair surprised me greatly at the time and I asked my friend if the child behaved this way often. I was even more surprised when she told me that she had never had occasion to prop up the bottle for her daughter before and that this was the first time she had refused to nurse in her arms. Some months later I asked this mother about the situation and she informed me that after the occasion I had witnessed, the child never again permitted herself to be held while being fed but had, henceforth, held the bottle from which she nursed until she gave it up entirely. There is no doubt that similar episodes are discoverable in the history of every infant. Of course, if one is not looking specifically for such events, they may never be noticed.

The ultimate solution to the *weaning paradox* generally involves a specific compromise. The libidinal component of the sucking instinct is repressed and only the nutritive function, now free of previous libidinal involvement, remains. This abandonment of the libinal component of eating signals the establishment of the primacy of the ego. In my descriptions and discussions I have made it appear that my model infant worked through the *weaning process* without great difficulty and passed smoothly and completely through each phase as the *infantile mode* of eating evolved into the *adult mode*. In fact, however, the completeness to which the *weaning process* is carried varies a great deal among individuals. The history of each *weaning process* is unique to each person.

Gross deviations of the *weaning process* preclude the attainment of a modicum of maturity and, as will be shown, significant distortions of the process form the foundation from which psychosis and other less severe forms of arrested maturity arise. Small areas of nonresolution of the paradoxes arising during the *weaning process can be* observed in everyday people. There follow descriptions of small pieces of behavior whose very existence, so far as I have been able to learn, has never before been discussed or recorded or, of course, explained. The rejection of *merging* does not appear to be an all-or-nothing response. Evidence for this can be seen in the behavior of adults in which traces of the *merging* pattern can be discerned. Indeed, it is only by calling upon this factor of behavior that certain events in life can be given meaning at all.

Occasionally, one may observe in himself or in others—especially in those close to him—a curious bit of staring behavior. The subject ceases all other activity and, though aware of all going on around himself, stares fixedly but without a special focus ahead of him, centering but not fixing his gaze on some object (the nature of which does not seem, as far as I can tell at this time, to have any particular significance). The subject is obviously "going through something" and that "something" is clearly gratifying, though one cannot define in words exactly, nor in what way, such behavior gratifies. The subject is far from being out of contact with the environment, yet he experiences a feeling of "suspended animation." Others, especially in the closeness of a family situation, may playfully attempt to "break up" this reaction. They may wave a hand in the line of vision without, however, diverting the subject's steadfast staring. They may push and jar him a bit, hard enough to evoke a "stop it!"—but the unwavering stare remains unaffected. He seems and feels entranced on an entirely voluntary basis, knowing full well that his "pose" can be instantly renounced should the need arise, but choosing to maintain it because of the mild pleasure it seemingly provides. It seems clear enough that this activity—this gazing—seems to be a "replay" of *raptus*. Perhaps some kinds of "day dreaming" represent similar derivations.

I think the term *raptus* can be used to advantage as an orientation to the further study of this previously unaccounted-for reaction. My observations are limited, but it has seemed to me that *raptus* reactions occur during periods of incorporative behavior. At mealtime, especially before breakfast is eaten, this reaction seems more prevalent than at other times of the day. And of course the dull, transfixed, unseeing gaze of the student ostensibly listening to a lecturing professor immediately suggests the *raptus* behavior I have described. It seems possible that what is commonly identified as "highway hypnosis" may actually be a *raptus* response, having its origins, of course, in experience unrecoverable by memory alone but evoked by the monotonous comfortableness of being filled with repetitive stimuli.

The second piece of everyday behavior to which I call attention is that displayed when one tastes some particularly delectable bit of food. The individual withdraws somewhat from others (in terms of relatedness) and holds his mouth in that unique position known only to him, calculated to enhance the pleasure he perceives. His eyes close partly or wholly for a moment and may "wander" for an instant or two. A modified expletive something between a grunt and a groan, conveys to those who witness the occasion how delightful and exceptional this particular sensory experience is to him. In our society, words to the effect of "Boy, is that good!" are many times spoken. I think it significant that such responses are found to be widely distributed outside our own culture and may very well prove to be universal. The details suggest to me that this, too, may be a brief "replay" of infantile experiences classifiable as *raptus* response.

To my way of thinking the phenomenon of "deja vu" has not yet been convincingly explained. It is difficult to study because of its rarity and the absence of data concerning the internal and external circumstances of a subject at the time of its occurrence. If one is going to consider it from the the clinical point of view, one must necessarily rely on what has been one's own experience. The phenomenon is so fleeting, and when it occurs is so engrossing, that the various parameters of the matrix in which the event takes place are not generally noticed. I have hoped to experience a deja vu (in order to study the phenomenon close at hand) but such has not occurred to me for many years. What I remember from the few occasions in the past when I had such experiences is fragmentary, but I believe I can recall the feeling tone I experienced as a curious kind of focusless stare, along with an effort to prolong the experience, presumably for the purpose of observing it more carefully, but actually, now that I look back upon it, for the purpose of continuing to enjoy a species of libidinal gratification. A strange place is always involved in deja vu, and in my personal experience an emptiness and a sense of loneliness seemed to be conditions related to its occurrence. In effect, the deja vu phenomenon presents an unknown situation as if it were familiar down to the finest details. Perhaps the very strangeness evokes the need to see the new scene as one with which one is on the most familiar terms. It seems to me that the phenomenon can be profitably interpreted as a "replay" of an infantile nursing experience, for it says in effect, "See, I am not empty and alone. Once again, as in my infancy, I am with fixed hypnotic gaze seeing a sight which is already quite familiar to me and, lo, I am filled." ("Filled," of course, by the experience itself, which has intruded upon and displaced what I had assumed to be an emptiness.)

There are cultures in which children long past the age of infancy continue to be suckled. These children go to the breast because it provides an easily available source of nutrient. *They do not merge, nor do they display raptus*: There are no random eye movements under half closed lids, there is no tremor response, and they do not "go out of this world" as they suckle. They do not feed according to the *infantile mode*, but have progressed to the *adult mode* wherein the libidinal concomitants of alimentation have been foresworn. Thus, even though such older children still obtain milk from their mother's breasts they are, nonetheless—as I have defined the term—weaned.

In American culture great emphasis is placed on the type of food the infant receives. A regular folklore, generated and supported by various sources, has grown up around infant feeding. What, if any, advantage accrues to feeding a newborn child "solids"—as is often done—is difficult to imagine. Perhaps some justification can be found from the nutritional point of view, or rarely from some sensitivity or allergy of the infant. Indeed, it is illusory to think of a child as eating "solid food" until it has developed teeth to a sufficient degree to reduce solids to a consistency that can be swallowed. The "solid" food the infant may be fed often is given in a bottle and has been processed to an extent where it physically resembles the milk it replaces. Such practices are not harmful to the infant—they may even be of value inasmuch as their employment is a constant reminder to the mother that the *adult mode* of eating is the one to which a premium is attached. The *adult mode* is not, however, to be confused with the techniques of feeding. A young infant *merges* and after a few months displays *raptus* when spoon fed as regularly as he would at breast or bottle.

From what has been said one can see that weaning is a

process characterized by a shift from one mode of eating to another; an observable transition from *infantile mode* to *adult mode*. Initially the infant *merges* during the entire period of his suckling. Gradually this behavior is replaced by a feeding period characterized by the blank, focusless *raptus* in the direction of the mother's face which, toward the end of each feeding, gives way to the already familiar *merging*. With time this unswerving gaze is gradually replaced by a purposeful, attentive eye contact with outside objects and a receptivity to outside stimuli. Indeed, the completion of the *weaning process* may frustrate the mother by virtue of the fact that the infant's attention is so easily diverted from the food she is trying to get him to eat!

The course taken by the weaning process is subject to a very great number of influences which cannot simply be designated "favorable" or "unfavorable." For example, consider the consequences when an infant contracts a "head cold." There is a dramatic effect upon his nursing. If the infant is quite young the disturbance is evident. The previous smooth working of the complex neuromuscular coordinated activity, which together we call "nursing," is shattered. The infant cannot breathe through his nose because it is "stuffed up," so he tries to breathe through his mouth. But his mouth is already fully occupied with suckling! The need for air takes precedence and he breaks the hold of his mouth on the breast and tries to take a breath. But there is milk in his mouth and his inhalation sets off the cough reflex which functions to protect the lungs from the entry of foreign objects. He takes the breath he needs and then takes the breast into his mouth. Only now he must exhale and since his nasal passages are closed, he has to relinquish his hold on the breast once more to exhale, and so on and on. If he suckles he cannot breathe and if he breathes he cannot suckle very effectively. It takes some degree of maturation to learn to suckle *and* breathe. It is interesting to speculate on what may be a confusing impression wrought upon the infant under this circumstance. In some persons, for example, the symptoms of a fear of suffocation seem to have their origins in just such occasions.

CHAPTER V

The Weaning Process
and
Ego Development

It has long been recognized that object representation not only accompanies but also originates in hunger. But curiously there is little available data regarding the psychophysiologic origins of the capacity to obtain gratification from objects but distantly related to that which satisfied the instinctual aim during early infancy. Or, to put the matter in somewhat more condensed form very little attention has been accorded the mechanism by which physiological activities acquire symbolic psychic representations. One conception of the psyche is based on the idea that there are psychic counterparts to physiological reactions having feedback effects upon the function of body organs. In this chapter the influence of the *weaning process* upon the origin and development of the ego will be considered. I shall approach the subject by examining in some detail the psychological transactions which take place when an infant suckles. When one observes a nursing infant his attention is drawn to the fact that the child, when thus engaged, presents an "image" having quite specific qualities not observable at other times.

After the first several weeks of life the contrast in appearance between the nursing and other states becomes undeniable. I refer once again to the details of the evolution of the infant's behavior during the weaning process described earlier. As each phase blends into the next, the details of the infant's behavior change, such modifications reflecting the influences of a growing ego upon responses which, in the beginning of life, are under reflex control.

A very young infant, in the first few weeks of his life, *merges* during an entire feeding. A three- or four-month-old infant displays *raptus* during the early portion of each feeding and *merges* only toward the latter's completion. With time *raptus* virtually replaces *merging*. When the *weaning process* has run its course, *raptus* itself is given up in favor of the *adult mode* of conduct while eating.

During the first few weeks of life the infant hardly possesses what we later designate an "ego." He has no awareness of himself as himself, nor can he distinguish one object in his environment from another, nor recognize himself as the possessor of an existence independent of others around him. He has not yet developed a reflective capacity and thus has no means by which he may distinguish what is real from what is unreal. Internal stimuli cannot be differentiated from external ones. His inherited constitution has provided him with oral sucking instincts which, being reinforced by anatomical, neurological, and libidinal elements, support his survival. Undoubtedly this state of affairs has come about as the consequence of selective evolutionary forces operative over uncounted generations.

During the early weeks of life the infant has not the slightest notion of what we adults consider cause-and-effect relationships. But the repetitive experience of hunger pangs relieved by suckling breast or bottle creates the circumstance wherein he differentiates one state of feeling from another. He establishes associations between these contrasting states of being and the means by which the one was transformed into the other. From this continuing experience of affective states being "determined" by external circumstances, the ego has its beginning.

Presumably, this early association of the empty feelings of hunger being assuaged by taking in through the mouth seems to be responsible for far-reaching psychological consequences in later times. The origin and development of the ego is intimately and inextricably interwoven with the *weaning process* because within the framework of the latter a large number of elemental associations and "logical" conclusions are achieved. A system of logic by which associations become interrelated in the psyche is developed. The rules of this logic are cast in a primitive form, more familiar to us in psychotic thinking where we find it pathognomonic. This form of logic is characterized by neglect of the factor of reality. The reader is doubtlessly familiar with this psychological feature, operating under the aegis of the pleasure principle. Though it has been called primitive thinking or magical thinking, I prefer the term *infantile logic* because of its reminder that the form of thought process referred to typifies preverbal mental life.

Infantile logic evolves from that first state of mind which has it that cause-and effect relationships are established when two events occur simultaneously or in close approximation with each other. It is the same kind of uni-dimensional logic prevalent in immature individuals irrespective of their chronological age. It seems possible to trace the evolution of logical thinking from the first primitive time-associated events in the infant's life to the conceptualizations of sophisticated people. The mark of ego maturity is the capacity to see that there are many "causes" of varying degree, significance, and influence which, in certain sequences, produce a host of "results," each of which can in turn serve causal function in a subsequent interaction. Because of the absence of reality-testing, three assumptions—on the strength of which the ego creates *infantile logic*—are conspicuous: (1) all things are possible and nothing is impossible; (2) the closer the temporal relationship between two events, the more firmly is the first occurrence considered as a "cause" of the second; (3) when events or objects fulfill an identical symbolic meaning they may be equated regardless of the real differences between them.

Infantile logic has, it must be recognized, a validity of

74

its own when operating within its limited framework. If the infant "theorizes" that his cry has the power to produce food, for example, he has the opportunity of "testing" the validity of this conception many times over. Ultimately he must modify his first ideas, for his increasing awareness of the world about him leads him to discover that milk is not offered to him simply because he cries. Thus, *infantile logic* is subject to the influences of reality as the infant's universe expands and is modified thereby. Furthermore, if the time lag between two events exceeds some critical figure, then *infantile logic* cannot establish any relationship between them on temporal grounds, but may, nonetheless, equate them when each has the same symbolic meanings in the unconscious.

As maturation proceeds the infant learns in this way to grasp the significance of factors not heretofore meaningful to him. The ego is forged out of such experiences. Appropriateness, that fittingness of behavior one expects from the mature adult, is beyond the infant's grasp. For adults, of course, logical thinking is quite automatic and the choices of possible etiological relationships do not have to be consciously weighed or considered because almost instantaneous retrieval and comparison of previous experience with a present one makes a realistic assessment relatively likely. But for the infant each experience is either entirely new or has but few relevant previously established associations stored in the memory bank. Consequently the infant is constantly faced with the problem of arranging his perceptions in relationship with each other. Out of this interaction of organism and environment the ego develops, from miniscule beginnings, an awareness of its own uniqueness and its own relative position in the real world. At about three months of age the ego begins to perceive what up to this time has gone unnoticed. It catches a glimpse of itself in a kind of psychic mirror, we might say, and from this time on the ego appreciates itself as a factor which must be taken into consideration along with all other circumstances in the infant's universe. This circumstance, of crucial importance to the ego's development, is signaled by a gradually increasing capacity to relate to other human beings as objects. The infant, becoming aware of his own unique individuality, begins to relate to others, manifesting this by his smile. This phenomenon comes to play an increasingly important role in ego function becoming an integral part of the latter's armamentarium in dealing with realities external to himself.

As the infant's ego becomes increasingly aware of itself, it accords itself an exalted place in the scheme of things. For his logical deductive activity leads him to the conclusion that he is the center of his universe. His experience supports the self-centeredness of this conception. Seeing himself as the power central to a universe where nothing is impossible, he considers that all his desires are achievable if only he can discover the appropriate formula. He never doubts, moreover, that such formulae exist. Nor, like the magical and superstitious practices which are lingering remnants of such *infantile logic,* need there be any real connection between the ritual and that which it is intended to produce or prevent. The infant seeks formulae by which the assumptions of *infantile logic* may be realized. His experience indicates that there are such devices. As he comes to understand it, crying brings his mother to him. His smile evokes hers. The "formulae" so familiar to us in obsessive-compulsive mechanisms reflects the preverbal origin of these patterns of psychological activity. One patient said to me, in this connection, that she was greatly disturbed because she had recurrent thoughts which she knew intellectually not to be true. She was obsessed with the idea that if something happened once it would quite likely happen again. As a consequence she developed magical formulae, one of whose functions was intended to prevent such "inevitabilities." Because, for example, she had had a minor auto accident immediately after turning to the right at a corner, she avoided a repeat performance of this accident by henceforth making only left hand turns! The practical difficulties and delays this engendered aside, the compulsion to behave this way is derived from the magical thinking process, which is abandoned as a psychological technique once maturity is achieved.

Infantile logic develops on a base of absolute ignorance of reality. The infant, with his fledgling ego, slowly develops the capacity to integrate current perceptions with the memory of earlier and similar sensory experiences. Almost everything that happens to him is "new." It will be some time before he can rigorously test the validity of his conceptions regarding his universe.

When this *infantile mode* of thinking is not put aside in adulthood the character is marked by credulousness. Credulous individuals treat unfamiliar occurrences as though they had never had any previous experience with which compare them. To them all things are possible; to declare the existence of an event or state of affairs is sufficient proof unto itself. For example, man declares that there are "flying saucers," and his answer to an opponent who requires more tangible proof than mere assertions is, "Prove they *don't* exist!"

As the infant's ego perceives more and more the events of his universe he begins their assemblage in what we may call a memory bank. The infant, in comparison with the adult, is at a disadvantage for he knows no words which can serve in his memory as stored symbols. The primitive memory, in contrast to that of the adult where word encoded experiences are retrievable long afterward, is a store of affects of the simplest kind. Furthermore, this circumstance puts the investigator of early psychological phenomena in the unenviable position of making interpretations without the possibility of the subject's verbal confirmation. There are no words retrievable and reportable in later life regarding preverbal experiences. But the affects are "remembered"—these affect memories are expressed as "moods" or "feeling tone."

Poets are more successful than others in reducing the incoherency of the latter experiences to a more readily communicated verbal form. The affect memories of early infancy do not lack intensity. Indeed, the very absence of verbal content seems to contribute to this characteristic. They are vague, indefinable, and but uncertainly associated with objects. A subtle estimate of their character and quality can be made by considering the "anxiety attack" with its free-floatingness and striking absence of verbal content. Once the anxiety becomes attached to content the intensity of anxiety diminishes. The acute anxiety attack in adult life can be considered a "replay" of specific weaning experiences evoked by circumstances which, when understood from the point of view of their symbolic meaning, tend to reproduce affect-evoking circumstances of early infancy. Once the "free-floating" anxiety acquires content, it can often be shown that the symbolic meaning of the now attached content is identical to the symbolic significance of the circumstance being "replayed." The matter is greatly complicated by the tendency for the manifest content to express unresolved conflicts from several levels of psychosexual development simultaneously.

In some respects a young infant's perceptions can be reckoned as dreamlike in character. The child applies *infantile logic* to the formulation of concepts about the relationships between events within and around him. He organizes, to some degree, an array of confusing and conflicting data, accomplishing this through the employment of *infantile logic* with its three assumptions. The formulations based upon the preverbal logic of "post hoc ergo propter hoc" begin long before speech is learned.

The infant, up to about three months of age, has *merged* each time he has nursed. At about this point in time, however, his developing ego comes to value its own existence so greatly that he "takes a second look" at the *merging* experience. For the first time the infant becomes aware that in *merging* he completely loses contact with himself. What had been no more than a matter of course in the infant's earlier "egoless" life now becomes, because of an increasing perceptual capacity, perceived as a threat of annihilation to the ego itself. Each time the infant *merges* it loses contact with its own ego. And, according to the reasoning of *infantile logic*, the one occurring in proximate relationship with the other is conceived to be the cause of the other. The infant develops, we might say, a "theory" by which to explain the psychological experience now associated with *merging*. The close temporal relationship between the gratification of suckling and the ego loss concomitant with that gratification "means" that there is a cause-and-effect connection between the two events. The infant's ego searches for a formula by which it can be preserved as a functioning entity while at the same time the gratifications of suckling and *merging* are maintained. In the process of maturing the ego has generated a paradox. If the child suckles and *merges* as he has always done, his just-barely-established ego boundaries appear to him to disintegrate. If he does not suckle he is assailed by increasingly intolerable waves of hunger and emptiness. Naturally the infant seeks a solution which satisfies both of these conflicting claims. And the solution the infant "hits upon," presumably on a trial and error basis, is the behavior I have named *"raptus."*

By such a strategem, infants shift their behavior away from the all-engulfing *merging* experience, the movement to *raptus* being sufficient to satisfy for a time an ego which is just beginning to exercise its finer critical qualities.

Through the maneuver of *raptus*, the ego seems to have achieved a state of "suspended animation" which now replaces the fragmentation of *merging* during the first part of a feeding session. The ego's demand that its own integrity be preserved has begun to force the relinquishment of *merging* while suckling. Gradually the time devoted to

79

raptus increases as the infant gets older and the periods of *merging* which occur at the termination of feedings decrease in length, and finally, when the *weaning process* has run its course, are given up altogether.

The ego's demands keep pace with its own development. It is not satisfied for very long with the compromise *raptus* offers. As its valuation of itself increases, so do its demands for its own mastery over circumstance. *Raptus,* the compromise to the weaning paradox, is no more than a temporizing solution. For it is inevitable that the expanding ego will "catch up" with *raptus* and find in it the same quality of threat to its continued existence as earlier *merging* presented. The *weaning paradox* has been shelved for the moment, a little nearer to solution than when first encountered. By degrees the earlier established patterns are forced to retreat under the impact of a progressively maturing ego. The net effect of the *weaning process* is observed when the infant renounces suckling according to the *infantile mode* and begins to eat according to the *adult mode.* Perhaps the definition of these modes bears repeating. The *infantile mode* is the term I employ to designate the manner in which psychological involvement of a libidinal character accompanies the mechanism of sucking; events previously described as *merging* and *raptus.* In contrast, the *adult mode* is the term I employ to designate the manner in which those who have completed the *weaning process* eat; where there is no *merging* and no *raptus.* In short, alimentation without libidinal involvement.

Weaning is a process which every infant experiences—not an event imposed upon him by the mother. As in any process which requires an elapsed time in which to be accomplished, it is subject to and shaped by many variables. Moreover, by assuming that the completeness to which the *weaning process* is carried out varies from one individual to another, an additional basis for psychological insights becomes available. The *weaning process* is long, and is subject to many vicissitudes between its commencement and its completion at about nine months.

The mother's technique of feeding her infant—whether by breast or bottle—her attitude towards her infant, the shape of the culture into which the infant is born—in short, the conditions under which the *weaning process* must operate—all have their influences. The infant's state of health and his general physical condition, the time of teething, and his intellectual endowment are likewise forces impinging upon the process. Perhaps a listing of the various factors arranged in order of relative importance will some day be possible despite the apparent oversimplification such a proposal promises.

The degree of weaning—the degree of shift from *infantile* to *adult mode* of behavior—is generally rather complete. But one should not assume that because the *adult mode* of eating has taken hold that no residuals of the *infantile mode* remain. Indeed, it seems to me that a great deal of adult immaturity is the consequence of a *weaning process* never carried to completion.

CHAPTER VI

THE WEANING PROCESS

Psychological Derivatives

A wide spectrum of phenomena, encompassing the most diverse manifestations, have their origins in the psychological compromises achieved during the weaning process. Classificatory schemes derived from the conception that psychological phenomena are either normal or abnormal, while practical enough for day-to-day clinical work, represent a species of dischotomous thinking too confining for investigational purposes. My concern is with the phenomenology of psychic events. The order in which I discuss them is arbitrary, no effort has been made to arrange them according to any hierarchy of significance.

The Orgasm

The psychophysiological origins of the orgasm are presently a matter of speculation. The fact of the orgasm has been accepted as self-explanatory and its genesis has not been thoroughly explored. The subject merits considerable study, in my opinion, considering the critical role disturbances in sexuality play in psychological disorders.

The orgasm is a psychophysiological event which seemingly makes its appearance around the time of puberty. That is to say, the capability for sexual climax becomes evident at this stage of maturation, though even here final judgment must be withheld because a sufficient amount of knowledge is not available regarding the role orgasm may play in prepubertal sexual activity.

The term "orgasm" is used quite loosely in psychological writings. Most who have written on the subject assume that the term is so well-known to the reader that no definition is required. Most of the emphasis in psychiatric writings has been devoted to the distinction discernible in the orgastic experiences in men contrasted to those in women; very little attention has been accorded to the similarities of orgasm in men and women.

It is helpful to consider the orgasm a process rather than viewing it simply as an event. The manifestations of the orgastic process differ according to the sex of the individual. The most obvious difference, of course, is the ejaculatory response which in the male accompanies orgasm. Then, too, there are perceptible but indescribable differences in experiences between one occasion of orgasm to another. That there are differences in the subjective response is commonly accepted, though the details are likewise unaccountable. Despite the prominence accorded to the characteristics of the male orgasm when contrasted to that experienced by the female, the process culminates in essentially identical psychophysiological states of relaxed satisfaction. Unhappily, disturbances of orgastic function are commonplace. By considering the phenomenon as a process rather than an instantaneous event, it is possible that deeper understanding of the nature of these psychophysiological malfunctions can be achieved.

I have had occasion, in treating patients, to learn something about the details of orgastic experience. I consider the following fragments of case material quite illuminating in view of the "idiom" in which the descriptions are couched. One woman described orgasm. "There is a sense of being all here. You may be here but your mind just loses control over your thoughts. It's just like a sense of enjoyment; contentment like a child fed at his mother's breast." Another woman, complaining of frigidity, described her difficulty as follows: "I don't lose myself—it's very short. I can't seem to let myself go."

A male patient had stated that his sexual capacity was "normal," that he had no difficulties of any kind. Yet when the matter was examined in detail it was discovered that, while from a mechanical point of view there were no discernible pathological elements, from the psychological side he performed the sex act with very little emotional involvement. Another man, plagued by premature ejaculation, tried holding off orgasm by repeating the multiplication table to himself during coitus. Though he did not say so, it seems obvious that his emotional participation in genital sexual behavior was virtually nil. A woman with psychological noninvolvement during coitus similar to the first man's would have been considered frigid both by herself and others, but because his ejaculatory capacity was unimpaired he considered himself "normal." This situation may be common and if so, frigidity may be as frequent a disorder in men as in women. Popular opinion has it otherwise, perhaps for the reason that in the minds of many, ejaculation is equated with orgasm. There seems to be a widespread belief that if the physiological mechanisms show no disturbance—if there is tumescence, ejaculation and detumescence—and if the time for performance lies within a reasonable range, the sexual function of the male is normal! In women the physiological accompaniments of orgasm are not so clearly delineated that they can be confused with orgasm proper. This fact alone may account for the widely held opinion that frigidity—i.e., the absence of emotional commitment during coitus—is predominantly a misfortune of women.

We are not, of course, trying to establish what is or is not "normal." Our interest is in the details of the orgasm; more specifically, the origins of the psychological components thereof.

There appear to be two principal components of the *orgasm process*. The first is physiological, manifested by rhythmic muscular activity directed toward accomplishing maximum penetration of the female sexual organ by that of the male. These penetrative movements are more or less subject to conscious control at the commencement of coitus, but with mounting excitation the rhythmicity generally passes beyond conscious control and becomes to all intents reflex in character. This in turn sets off rhythmic contractions of the pelvic musculature, producing ejaculation in the male and rhythmic contractions of the vaginal wall in the female. Detumescence and sleep usually follow. This describes the physiology of orgasm in general terms.

In addition, there is a second component—the psychological aspect—to consider. As the voluntary rhythmic muscular activity assumes the character of a reflex activity, this may or may not be accompanied by the following very specific psychological phenomena. As the climax is approached the participants "lose themselves." Their ego contact with objects progressively fades until there is a mutual *merging*. For these few moments the ego boundaries simply do not exist and the "oneness" between lovers, of which the poets write, becomes a reality. This response is not a loss of consciousness; it has a distinctly different quality therefrom and is accompanied by a sense of fulfilled gratification not satisfactorily reducible to terms of the spoken or written language.

Once, when I asked the mother of an infant in arms to describe as graphically as she could the reaction she observed when her child nursed, I received the following reply: "He's just not there any more—just like he's lost. I've always thought that is the way an orgasm ought to be . . . just being completely out of it." The comparison seems suggestive of the idea that the *merging* which characterized the early phase of the *weaning process* may be standing in the wings, as it were, waiting its turn to come on stage once more long after the *adult mode* of behavior has been established. It is hard to see how the comparison of the infant's oblivion while nursing to the emotion experienced during orgasm could be improved upon. It is especially impressive because the individual questioned spontaneously associated the *merging* of the infant with the orgasm of the adult. And even though it may seem to be a fanciful or even incredible suggestion, I think the theory that the orgastic experience of the adult has its origins in the *merging* response during early infancy deserves serious consideration.

Frigidity is a disorder characterized, in my opinion, by various degrees of incapacity to *merge* with a sexual partner during the moment of sexual climax. The extent and degree of *merging* seems to vary from one experience of coitus to another. Much depends upon factors ranging from physical well-being to love for the partner.

If, during the *weaning process,* the fear of *merging* is not resolved, it will seriously inhibit and may prevent altogether the *merging response* during coitus in adult life. Variants of such inhibitions are extremely frequent, and altogether are probably responsible for more unhappiness than any other single area of psychological disturbance.

The reader will recall the *tremor response* which was touched upon briefly in a previous chapter. The ultimate fate of this physiological reaction is its reappearance at the moment of climax during coitus. One man said to me in this connection, "Doctor, I don't know what's wrong with me, When I have an orgasm I sometimes shiver all over just like a wet dog."

The *quiver response* and *merging* which "disappear" as the *weaning process* proceeds from the *infantile mode* of eating to the *adult mode,* have not disappeared at all. Under relentless pressures of the maturing ego the *merging* response is repressed, only to reappear during the orgasm. The genital apparatus takes over the executive function once performed by the oral structures. What is forbidden in the oral idiom is licit in the genital syntax. This shift to genitality is the hallmark of sexual maturity. To put the matter into psychoanalytic terminology: libido discharged by oral executive organs during infancy becomes the serant of genital sexuality in maturity. From this it becomes obvious that disturbances of orgastic potency have for their primary genesis an incompleteness of the *weaning process*. Disturbances producing distortions of the *weaning process* form the framework to which conflicts occurring during the latter periods of psychosexual development attach themselves. For it will be observed that all disturbances of orgastic potency, whether in men or women, have in addition to unresolved conflicts of a specific sexual nature, important components derived from incomplete resolution of the *weaning process*. The difficulty is invariably some form of reluctance to *merge* with a love object, a reluctance manifested variously, but always functioning to negate anxiety attached to *merging*. Where *merging* during coitus is inhibited, only partial discharge of the sexual instincts can be achieved. It is the failure to completely discharge sexual tensions that we designate "frigidity." While the diagnosis of frigidity is made in women often enough, it is almost never made in men! Clinically, men do not always complain if, in the course of sexual relations, they do not *merge* with their love objects. They often emphasize the physical aspects of the sexual act, confusing ejaculation with the total experience of the *orgasm process*. If erection is maintained and ejaculation achieved, this is taken as proof of orgastic potency. The demand is infrequently made of the man by his partner that he *merge* with her. Because of the evolutionary history of the *merging* response which long after the *weaning process* has been completed finds a pathway for expression acceptable to the ego during coitus, any residual unconscious fears associated with *merging* are evoked by the orgasm process. In my experience orgastic pathology, however presented to the clinician, is ultimately traceable to anxieties first encountered during the *weaning process*.

Perhaps no psychological phenomenon is less understood nor more important in its implications for medicine than hallucination. The subject has been compartmentalized, a methodological necessity in view of the absence of a theory explaining hallucination in the same terms as other psychological events. There is, for example, the conception that hallucinations are invariably pathological and indicate psychosis; this idea coexists with the concept that hallucinations are almost to be expected of lost explorers, individuals by no means to be considered psychotic. The journals of Artic explorers, sailors, and desert travelers not infrequently refer to hallucinatory experiences. Hallucination experienced within a religious frame of reference is even more familiar. Hallucinatory experiences of different kinds, by virtue of the fact that they have not been correctly identified as such, masquerade in various guises and have been ascribed to different causes. So there is sufficient reason for considering the subject of sensory perceptions experienced in the absence of demonstrable objective "cause."

Several approaches to the subject are possible. I have chosen to consider the phemenon of hallucination from the point of view of the psychic economy. For this reason the sensory modality through which they are perceived, and the ideational content when such there be, are less significant than the functional role hallucinations of every kind are created within the psyche to perform. In my judgment, the form, content, and sensory modality of hallucination are the servants of the phenomenon. Hallucinations I find, have a general function they invariably fulfill wherever they occur. They also serve, within this framework, psychic requirements unique for each person. Identical functions are served by phenomena as seemingly diverse as dreams and those sensory disturbances known as "psychosomatic symptoms" in medical practice. The latter are but varying manifestations of hallucination.

Hallucination may be defined as a conscious awareness of sensory perceptions for which no objective physical stimuli are demonstrably present. They occur in all modalities of sensation, either singly or in various combinations thereof. Hence a listing of the modalities of sensory experience would coincide with a catalogue of hallucinatory phenomena. No modality of sensation is exempt as a channel through which hallucination may be perceived. To come to the conclusion that a man who complains of "hearing voices" is hallucinated is an easily agreed upon diagnosis. But where the sensory experience has no verbal content or is vague and indescribable, it is not always easy to recognize the latter as hallucinatory. If experiences occurring in the absence of physical stimuli are to be comprehended as hallucinations, one must acknowledge that all sorts and kinds of sensations, painful or otherwise, for which demonstrable physical cause cannot be established, may be hallucinatory. The diagnosis of hallucination is *not* to be made by the exclusion of other causes for a particular sensation. As will be developed, there are specific circumstances requisite to their occurrence and specific clinical characteristics by which they may be identified.

We are examining the idea that all functional sensory complaints, no matter where they are located anatomically and regardless of their manner of presentation, are but variants of the same phenomenon: hallucination. This seems a bold suggestion, for it means that no less than 70% of patients who present themselves to physicians with aches, pains, headaches, dizziness, paresthesias, and other sensory complaints for which no physical cause is evident, may be experiencing hallucinations. Let us examine the matter in more detail.

The first task, it seems to me, is to clear up the confusing concept that hallucination is experienced by everyday people *and* is diagnostic of psychosis. Is it true that hallucinations are signs and symptoms of psychosis? It is true enough that they are discoverable as part of the clinical picture in many of those who are chronically psychotic, and in most of those who are acutely so. But this is not the same as saying that hallucinations themselves are diagnostic of psychosis! I think the evidence is well-established that hallucinatory experiences are by no means confined to those who are psychotic.

I have investigated some aspects of hallucinations. As a consequence of these studies I have concluded that hallucinatory experiences are encountered with considerable frequency in ordinary people, and that they may be benign and without psychopathological implications. In my opinion the paradox is solved by considering that it is not the phenomenon of hallucination which is pathological, but the manner in which the ego deals with the perception that decides the matter.

The most commonplace hallucination in everyday life is that experienced while one sleeps; i.e., dreams. This phenomenon fulfills all the criteria of the definition for hallucination, and the fact that it occurs in sleep rather than during the waking state does not alter in any way the hallucinatory nature of the experience. Nor can the sleep state vs. the waking state serve to demarcate dream from other hallucinatory phenomena. For at times the hallucination commencing while one sleeps continues even after full consciousness has been achieved! The mature ego deals with the sleeping hallucination as it does with the waking hallucination. The content of the dream experience is characteristically repressed shortly after one wakes. More often than not the dream content does not reach consciousness and then, of course, cannot be recalled when one awakes. When the hallucination occurring during sleep is recalled upon awaking, it is unusual for one to remember its content for very long; all that remains is the remembrance of having had such an experience. Hallucinations occurring in everyday waking life are dealt with summarily by prompt repression so that their content—when there is content is no more retrievable than the content of dreams after a lapse of time.

"But," the reader may ask, "what about a normal person like myself? Dreams? Yes, I've had them and maybe they are hallucinations while asleep. But I've searched my memory and I can find no such experiences while awake. I've never 'heard voices' nor 'seen visions' nor do I recall any body sensation which was not explainable on a physical basis." Such a response is to be expected, both in the light of what I have said about repression which such experiences normally undergo, and the conventional pattern of our culture which prejudges such psychic phenomena as pathological. And of course most of us wish to be "normal."

In the course of my investigation of hallucinatory experiences I have asked many ordinary people if they have ever heard "voices." I have invariably received an initial denial from them. But when I persisted and subsequently posed the same question in the form of, "Have you ever had the experience of hearing your name called only to discover that there was no person present other than yourself?" affirmations were readily obtained. And if, seeing my interest, the individual warmed to the subject, he might relate hallucinatory experiences going beyond this prosaic example.

Knowledge of the ubiquity and variety of hallucinatory experience is of special value to physicians. Knowing of it, doctors are in a position to allay the considerable anxiety evoked by hallucinations occuring under circumstances where the culture equates their presence with "being crazy." Incidentally, in those American subcultures where ignorance and superstition are the rule, hallucinations are much more readily acknowledged than among the more civilized. "God" can say a few words to you in Appalachia, but one dare not acknowledge such apparitions even to oneself in a university setting.

In earlier publications I limited myself almost entirely to the study of hallucinated auditory and visual phenomena. Since then I have encountered an abundance of data confirming the idea that all people hallucinate in all modalities at one time or another. What distinguishes the sick from the healthy is the mode in which the phenomena are dealt with by the ego. One brief case in point is that the dreams of those with psychosis cannot be differentiated on the basis of content from hallucination occurring during the sleep of normal people.

In contrast to the mature ego's method of dealing with hallucination, whether experienced in the waking or sleeping state, the immature ego becomes preoccupied with sensory experiences it perceives. Where the normal person forgets that he has even had the experience of hallucination, the immature builds and elaborates the experience, which continues to fill his waking thoughts and becomes the center of all his attention. The hallucination becomes subject, by the immature ego, to an elaborative process through which what begins as a hallucination expands and develops into a delusion—itself a psychic phenomenon often subject to further extension and organization.

In psychosis the ruminative activity of the immature ego maintains the existence of hallucination. One must not confuse hallucinatory content, where such is present, with the phenomenon itself. The content is determined by unconscious conflictual material from all levels of psychosexual development, more especially from those which evolve after the acquisition of speech. The immature ego molds the hallucination to its own requirements. In the course of this working-over the hallucination acquires content which in turn becomes distorted according to unconscious psychic requirements and progresses to that organization of thought which we call delusion. In my opinion every delusion originates in hallucination.

A patient of mine served in the army as a clerk-typist. One day he "heard" a comment about himself. Catching sight of two men talking with each other he immediately explained the otherwise inexplicable auditory hallucination by ascribing to them the source of a derogatory remark. The delusion formed so quickly after the hallucination that for practical clinical purposes they can be considered together.

The explanation for the observed fact that delusions may exist without concurrent and accompanying hallucination is, I believe, that delusion requires a lower level of energy expenditure than is required to produce hallucination. Delusion has the advantage of content. It appeals to the intellect and demonstrates the effort of the ego, albeit an unsuccessful one, to bring anxiety under control. A delusion, in my judgment, is a steadier crutch to the disorganized and immature ego than the hallucination from which it arose. It must be emphasized that delusion and its parent, hallucination, perform precisely identical functions in the psyche. They both serve, in their own fashion, to fill what would otherwise be an intolerable psychic void.

Under circumstances of isolation and emptiness, normal people may hallucinate quite extensively. I recall reading an account of a man and wife whose car had broken down in an isolated desert area. Both were dead when they were finally discovered. The wife had kept a diary of the happenings of the tragic misfortune they endured. They had no water or food with them, and no means of obtaining any. After two or three days both experienced visual hallucinations. The wife "saw" a peddler approaching with a pack on his back; the husband "saw" telegraph lines in the distance. The chronicler and her husband were both aware of the hallucinatory character of their experiences, she wrote, yet there was a very "real" quality to the experience for both of them.

I think it likely that in psychosis the ego relinquishes an already inadequate function of discovering outside objects, which keeps a flow of afferent stimuli directed toward itself. Instead, the obligatory requirement for stimuli is satisfied from inner sources ever ready to fill a void. Delusions—that is, convictions which, besides being beyond the influence of reason, have no validity in reality—are traditionally thought of as psychotic phenomena. Indeed, it is traditional in psychiatry to consider delusions pathognomonic of psychosis. The corollary to this thought is that normal people do not entertain delusions! In fact, however, delusions seem to be as much a part of everyday life as the hallucinations from which they develop. This, naturally, is a startling claim, standing as it does in direct contradiction to what most people assume to be true. Well, clearly there is *some* difference that distinguishes the sane from the insane. And if it is not to be found here—where we have always believed it to reside—then where does the distinction lie? The reader, I feel sure, has observed that I have not dealt with the content of delusion but have considered the subject entirely from the phenomenological point of view.

The function of delusion is precisely to rationalize or serve the hallucination from which it is an extension. Delusion is an attempt to organize and subjugate hallucinatory experience to the control of the ego. This is why, during the acute phase of psychosis when ego disorganization is at its heights, that hallucination is often florid and is experienced within an aura of confusion, anxiety, and loss of reality contact. When the ego begins to reassemble its boundaries the beginnings of delusion can sometimes be observed. The patient no longer hears unidentifiable, incoherent "voices"—as he perhaps had at the onset of ego dissolution—but instead will hear a man's voice accusing him of using his mouth for perverse practices. And when further ego reintegration takes place, the voices are no longer perceived. Meanwhile, the patient has extended the delusion to embrace the conviction that the F.B.I. is persecuting him by constantly spying on him. With the passage of time the delusion may be elaborately organized and supported by an extensive system of circumstantial evidence, credible in the eyes of the patient and occasionally to others as well.

We shall now consider some of the psychological consequences of the *weaning process* in detail. The reader will recall that hunger is cyclic; the pangs of hunger are attributable to hunger contractions originating in the cardia of the stomach. From small beginnings these muscular contractions increase in both amplitude and frequently until, breaking through the pain barrier, they reach consciousness, where they are perceived as hunger pangs. Food entering the stomach terminates these hunger contractions, but gastric physiology is such that even in the absence of food the hunger contractions decrease in intensity and frequency and, for a time, hunger is not experienced. This is the cyclic phenomenon, it will be recalled, to which I gave the name *hunger tide*.

Infants cry when they experience hunger pangs. This behavior is universal; for an infant not to react in such manner would be unthinkable. The effect of an infant's hunger cry on adults, especially those charged with his care, requires no description. But what about the effect upon the crying infant himself? It has been demonstrated that even while in utero the fetus will display movement in response to sound waves. And after birth a sharp loud sound will elicit muscular reflex behavior in normal infants. From these findings we know that the mechanism for auditory perception is in working order in the newborn. We must suppose that, having auditory capability, the infant cannot help but perceive sound. Of all the sounds around him, of all the unintelligible noise that impinges on his auditory apparatus, *his own cry* must be a frequent and unavoidable perception. He hears his own cry reflected back to him from the surfaces of the room and its contents. And the sound of his voice reaches his ear by direct air transmission as well as by bone conduction. Visual stimulation may be shut out by closing the eyes, tactile sensations almost eliminated from perception by remaining motionless, but auditory sensations are obligate and cannot be avoided. There is, moreover, a precise relationship actually present between two perceptions: the pangs of hunger and the sound of his own cry. The infant, through the application of *infantile logic,* formulates the interpretation that there is a specific relationship between hearing his own cry and the pangs of hunger which he perceived as occurring in close temporal relationship. In a manner of speaking, a cause-and-effect theory is established on the basis of this association. From the infant's viewpoint perhaps the situation can be approximated as follows: "When I hear the sound of my own cry, milk comes and relieves my hunger." But we know that the infant's hunger dissipates even though he is not fed when, by his cry, he signals his discomfort. For, even though he is not nursed, his hunger abates as the *hunger tide* ebbs. So to the *infantile theory* that his cry calls forth milk which causes hunger to disappear is added a second "conclusion," namely, "My crying causes the hunger to vanish." In effect, the infant comes to understand the circumstances as follows: "I felt hunger and cried. As I heard the sound of my own voice the feeling of hunger disappeared. Therefore, my cry serves the same function as milk." Through the operation of *infantile logic* the child develops the conception that the sensory stimulus of his own self-generated cry is, like food, capable of ending the discomfort of his emptiness. This "theory" undergoes further modification as experience demonstrates its incorrectness. Of course, the "memory" of such a connection between the sound of his own voice and the ebbing away of hunger pangs is retained. Such a "theory," having once been formulated by the ego, is subsequently repressed or tucked away in the memory bank as more complete "theories" replace it.

It seems probable, in my judgment, that such a situation is experienced by all infants, no matter how attentive or concerned a mother might be. I have personally observed an infant obviously crying in hunger refuse the proffered bottle and then, after a lapse of time, give up crying and fall asleep—just as would have occurred had the bottle been taken. Reduced to its simplest terms, the equation hunger cry = milk becomes a part of the symbolic content of the psyche. But perhaps this is all no more than fanciful thinking; an exercise in mental gymnastics. It is an interesting hypothesis, but how does the conclusion jibe with observation? After all, the infant can communicate nothing of this to us in words. Perhaps the idea that he correlates the sound of his own voice with the taking in of milk and with the relief of feelings of emptiness is nothing more than retrospective assignment of adult capabilities to an infant in arms.

If, as I have postulated, the perception of a "voice" comes to function as an agent which "fills" an otherwise painful void or emptiness, one should expect to find clinical correlates of such a relationship.

My studies on the effect of a variety of oral activities on hallucination confirm the existence of the postulated relationship. Oral activities of all kinds, eating and drinking especially, have profound effects upon hallucination, usually in the direction of abolishing the phenomenon for a time altogether. One must assume that once the *infantile theory* has been established, that the sound of one's own voice functions to fill emptiness after the manner of milk. The function the hallucination serves through the auditory modality comes to be served by all other sensory modalities as well. This further development follows the format of *infantile logic* already discussed. Each modality of sensation is equated with every other modality of sensation by virtue of the fact that they share in common the channeling of stimuli to the central nervous system. The confusion between modalities of sensory perception are quite easily seen in haptic hallucinations. Here, it will be recalled, "voices are seen," "visions are heard," etc. Though more obscure, the descriptions provided by patients of somatic hallucinations very often manifest the same phenomenon of the equability of one modality of perception with all others. If auditory perceptions fill the function

97

that milk does, then olfactory, gustatory, visual and somatic sensory perceptions can likewise fill what would otherwise be emptiness.

In my judgment, experimental studies on sensory deprivation lend support to the theory I have advanced to explain the function hallucination plays in the psyche. It has repeatedly been shown that man is stimulus-hungry and when deprived of the filling eflect of sufficient stimuli external to himself, he hallucinates to fill the void. The content of an auditory hallucination is often, but not invariably, verbal and therefore communicable, but hallucinatory experiences in the other modalities can hardly be reduced to meaningful verbal terms. In my opinion the significance of hallucination resides in the function it performs in the psyche.

One can hardly discuss hallucinations without making some comment on the important topic of hallucinogens. From my small knowledge (some years ago R.D. Goldner and I published the results of our study of the physiological effects of L.S.D) I would estimate that all hallucinogens—and there are a great many pharmacological substances in this category—evoke (rather than cause) hallucinations, since the drug effects differ quite widely in individuals and even in the same individuals at different times and under different conditions. I think it likely that there is a correlation between the readiness to hallucinate and ego maturity. For it is strikingly evident that hallucinatory experiences are sought by the more immature, an observation entirely in support of the theory of hallucination. I estimate that the hallucinogens create, through chemical means, a state of being that is analogous to that experienced by the hungry infant. Descriptions of L.S.D. intoxication, even couched as they are in sometimes mystical frames of reference, sound very much like what one might imagine an infant experiences when he *merges*. The expression, "take a trip"—referring of course to the L.S.D. experience—further suggests the picture of a young infant suckling. To say that as he suckles he "takes a trip" is in every way as satisfactory an expression to describe what transpires as to say he "merges."

Placebo

The discovery of the effect of oral activity on hallucination suggests the essential psychophysiological factors responsible for the phenomenon of the placebo effect. Since antiquity it has been known that pharmacologically inactive substances, when administered as "medicine," may prove to be therapeutic, abolishing or ameliorating those symptoms which led the sufferer to seek remedy. The word "placebo" means literally "I shall please." According to the dictionary such a substance is administered "merely to humor the patient." But the definition is insufficient, I think. I prefer to consider "placebo effects" to be those consequences of drug administration unrelated to the pharmacological properties of the preparation. The placebo effect has played a sizable role in medicine since time immemorial. The dictionary limits the scope of its definition to those probably rare occasions when the physician knowingly attempts to placate rather than cure. The placebo effect, of course, operates without relationship to the conscious intention of the physician, whether it be to please or otherwise. Its influence is specifically determined by whatever total symbolic significance the placebo has for the subject. The number of "proven effective" medicinals from past ages are legend. Included among them are many preparations either demonstrably harmful or pharmacologically inactive. In other words, "proven effective" drugs having no real influence on the pathological process they were supposed to favorably affect, have been employed from the earliest times in the treatment of all manner of disease and the relief of all types of symptoms. Their efficacy is not to be doubted but to be understood. It was their placebo effect that "cured."

Nor is the placebo effect limited to the administration

of medicaments. There is no procedure undertaken in the name of "treatment" which is exempt from the placebo effect. Indeed, not a few modes of therapy owe what efficacy they enjoy to this alone. At one time, for example, delivering the patient of a varying number of ounces of his blood was earnestly believed to be excellent therapy for most illnesses. The procedure was on this account highly regarded and frequently resorted to. Today we know that the medical indications for this procedure are limited to a very few pathological conditions and is rarely indicated. Medications which prove efficacious in one era do not necessarily retain their effectiveness. There are fashions in medicine. What is effective as medical procedure in one century or culture may prove useless in another.

It has been suggested that placebos are effective through "suggestion," but the matter is generally left to rest there without discussion as to the mechanics by which the suggestion becomes operative. One should not expect placebos to be effective in illnesses whose origins are organic, of course. Yet, curious to relate, some organic illnesses do respond to therapies which rely upon the placebo effect. (The practitioners of acupuncture, chiropractic and homeopathy are unknowing beneficiaries of this fact.) The mystery posed by this observation yields to comprehension when one recognizes that all illnesses or disfunctions, even those attributable to organic origins, display superimposed psychological factors. The functional components of the symptom complex having yielded to the placebo effect, the impression is created that an illness thought to be entirely due to organic malfunction has been favorably influenced by the placebo. By the same token, all substances and procedures administered or undertaken with avowed therapeutic aim have potential placebo components whether or not they are recognized as possessing such. The effect resides not in the substance or procedure, but in the unconscious of both patient and physician and the expectation related to the "treatment" contemplated.

The placebo effect is found only in man. Animals, having psychological mechanisms far more primitive than man, do not react to one substance as though it might be another! For this reason the placebo effect is unknown in veterinarian medicine. The one essential condition for the production of the placebo effect is the subject's conviction that whatever steps are taken, they will have an effect upon him. This effect, by the way, may be in either a negative or positive direction.

The mystery of the placebo effect—the mechanism whereby an active medicament or even chalk or milk sugar produces an alteration of sensory symptoms—can be related to the foregoing considerations. One observes that it is the sensory side of the complaint which changes when a placebo exercises its effect. And this alteration in sensory perception is the consequence of incorporation. And, since it has already been indicated that hallucination is identically influenced by oral incorporative activity, it follows that what has been affected is a hallucination. The symptoms influenced by the administration of placebo medication are now identifiable as somatic hallucinations. Recalling the fact that hallucinations of all kinds are ameliorated by oral activity—especially eating and drinking—the reason for the placebo response is found to be that the latter "fills" the painful void more economically and with greater symbolic relevance than the sensory symptom which it replaced. Furthermore, I think we can now correctly and accurately identify the essential hallucinatory nature of what modern medicine refers to as "functional" complaints. On many occasions, however, medication is administered by other than the oral route. And while it seems logical enough to explain the mechanism of placebo response where the prescription is given by mouth, the reasoning is not so easily followed where an injected medication is employed by the physician. The objection must be answered for an "injection" does not constitute an oral activity in its usual sense any more than does a surgical tying-off of the internal mammary artery (a procedure for the relief of angina which is clearly effective because of the placebo effect, the anatomical relationship between the heart and the artery being non-existent despite the close spatial relationship). Afferent stimuli are "taken into" the central nervous system via the receptor nerves. By the operation of *infantile logic,* everything that is taken in by any route whatever is equated with the first experience of "taking in"—the suckling of milk. Thus the formula that oral activity affects hallucination can be extended by rephrasing the matter thusly: Incorporative activity influences hallucinations, usually diminishing their intensity or abolishing the phenomenon altogether. When a person is given an injection he becomes the receptor of a medicinal substance which he "takes in" or incorporates. It is the incorporation that is important, not the portal of entry through which the incorporation is achieved.

Just as the hunger pangs of the infant were relieved either by taking in food or, according to *infantile logic,* by hearing his own cry, so the hallucinatory components of disease are likewise affected by a substance or procedure which has become symbolically equated with milk in the unconscious. The placebo effect, as has been suggested, is not always in an ameliorative direction when a drug is administered or a therapeutic manipulation undertaken. Indeed, if it were not for the placebo effect and the unending search for the certain "something" that relieves—as during infancy milk relieves the infant's discomfort—the giant pharmaceutical industry would likely be many times smaller than it is!

Depression

Depressive reactions are customarily classified as to subtype: "reactive depression," where the examiner understands the reaction to be in response to an identifiable event; "endogenous depression," where an external reason

102

for the reaction is not discoverable; and "postpartum depression," where depression follows the birth of a child. There are also "psychoneurotic depressions" and "psychotic depressions." Within the various entities there are varying degrees of involvement of the ego. In addition there is the depressive reaction which, because it is specifically attendant upon the death of a loved one, is given the special designation, "mourning."

Depressive reactions are manifested by psychological and physiological symptoms and ofttimes by somatic complaints. The psychological symptoms cluster about pessimistic ideas the sufferer entertains about himself and the world. These can run the gamut from a mild discouragement to a profound apathetic conviction of utter worthlessness. These feelings fluctuate in intensity during the course of a depressive reaction, and even during the patient's best moments are lying in wait to spring upon him. The most prominent feature of the fantasy life of depressed people is their preoccupation with the idea of their own death, by old age, suicide, accident, or disease.

The physiological symptoms generally appear as loss of appetite and weight, wakefulness, constipation. On the psychological side there is loss of sexual desire, frigidity, impotence, and a general decrease in the capacity for all conscious libidinal gratification. The somatic symptoms present themselves in so many anatomical locations that no contribution to their understanding would be afforded by cataloguing them. Though complaints arising from the somatic components of depressive reactions are limitless, both as to the kind of discomfort experienced and the anatomical site of that discomfort, there is a tendency for these to cluster about some portion of the gastrointestinal tract.

When the patient's motivation to learn about himself is sufficiently strong to enable us to consider the psychological symptoms in some detail, we find in every instance that *the individual has experienced some kind of loss*, the experience of said loss being directly relatable to the origin of the depressive symptoms. The loss may be as obvious as the death of a relative or friend, or it may be the "loss" of the individual's dreams of success which collapsed when a hoped-for event did not materialize. The The correlation of "loss" to a depressive reaction is so high that when such is not discoverable, the loss may be either too subtle to be appreciated by the investigator, or too trivial in the latter's judgment to be genetically significant, or too insignificant in the *examiner's* view to be given credence.

A young woman came to me because of the sudden onset of depression three months after the birth of her first child. Her illness could not be diagnosed as a postpartum depression because this invariably occurs within a few days after delivery. Moreover, in these instances the unconscious of the individual conceives of the birth of a child as a "loss" to the mother of an object she has had growing within her body for the preceding nine months. The "gain" of having an infant, obvious enough to the adult intellect, does not impress the unconscious nor does it offset the "loss" in women predisposed to depressive reactions. This young woman's depressive symptoms began when she ceased breast feeding her child. The "loss" she had sustained was the feeling she had experienced for three months following delivery. During that period she had appreciated a deep sense of importance and worth that she had not known prior to the child's birth. When, because the infant's demand for food was greater than her milk supply, she simply stopped nursing him at the breast and switched (over the protests of the baby) to bottle feeding, she became depressed. Nor could the restoration of breast feeding have reversed the depressive response, even after the onset of depression. For once established the depressive symptoms serve to fill the psychic void attendant upon the preceding "loss." And because depressive symptoms are close at hand—because they are immediately at the beck and call of the sufferer—the filling function they serve is attainable more easily, and with less expenditure of energy, than filling experiences whose origins lie beyond the bodily boundaries of the individual.

The somatic symptoms of depression are frequently confounded with the symptoms of organic disease. So common are depressive reactions, with or without the conscious awareness of the subjective feelings of depression that organic disease is often considered the most likely origin. For many years I have used the term "depressive equivalent reaction" to describe those depressive reactions where an otherwise subjective depression manifests itself instead in "somatic language." It helps, I think, to employ such terminology if for no other reason than it reminds one that the manifestations of depression may assume somatic guises. The distinction between "depressive equivalent reaction" and organic disease is not so readily established by the psychiatrist if a history of a "loss" of some kind cannot be elicited and correlated with the onset of symptomatology.

In the case of depression following on the heels of giving up breast feeding just mentioned earlier, a hint was offered as to the replacement function the symptoms served in the patient's psychic economy. It remains but to apply this concept to the symptomatology of depressions in general. The function of depressive symptoms is to fill what would otherwise be a painful sense of emptiness and loss. Its advent is designed to restore that which has been lost. Where the "reverse of the coin" mania predominates, it can hardly be questioned that the symptoms fill consciousness with a plethora of stimulae. This function of filling is independent, in my opinion, of whatever verbal content the depressive symptom may possess. Preoccupation with feelings of sin or unworthiness, for example, fill in the hiatus created by the loss. It is the advent of this loss that signals the onset of depressive equivalent symptomatology. Aches and pains of every kind fill the sufferer's thoughts and feelings so that other less intense mental occupations are forced aside. While basic to the symptomatology of depression— which in my experience does not occur without a loss of something the sufferer considers in his unconscious essential to him—the reaction serves as a vehicle for psychodynamics, with which the reader is already familiar.

Whereas the fundamental functions performed by the somatic and the psychological symptoms of depression are relatively simple and straightforward, the psychodynamics of physiological symptoms are more complex. The loss of zest, appetite, and decrease of food intake accomplishes at one stroke a number of simultaneous unconscious aims. It must be recognized that the "loss" of an object which initiates the depressive reaction (itself a psychic maneuver to replace that loss) uncovers a long dormant incorporative urge dating back to early infancy. The ambivalent attitude of the depressed person toward the resurgent oral incorporative impulse he experiences recalls the *weaning paradox* wherein resolution is sought to the conflict inherent in the *infantile mode* of conduct. The loss of appetite follows upon the patient's being already "filled" by symptoms, at the same time that it seems to deny emphatically every wish to incorporate. Indeed, it can be considered that the symptom "protests too much." By the same token, wakefulness seems to express mutually incompatible aims. On the one hand the continued awareness of sensory input is assured; on the other the infantile urge to relinquish ego control as in the *merging* response is denied.

In brief then, unsatiated primitive hunger impulses are exposed by an object loss having specific symbolic meaning to the depressed person. To better relate the depressive reactions to the earliest time of life I refer back now to that experience encountered during the *weaning process* where, because of *merging* and *raptus*, the ego, fearing for its integrity, shifted from the *infantile mode* to the *adult mode* of consuming food. In those who become depressed

106

in later life, renunciation of oral *merging* has been incomplete. It is an though lip service has been paid to the necessity of relinquishing the *infantile mode* but the commitment to the *adult mode* has been less than complete. The stress of an orally symbolic object loss strains the defenses which have, up to this time, held back the primitive oral wishes with relative success. The ego, as a consequence of being deprived of its gratification, retreats to a more primitive means by which the latter can be obtained. The significance of appetite and eating disturbances is so great in depressive reactions that the dynamics deserve recapitulation.

The refusal to eat, or what amounts to much the same thing—the inhibition of the capability to enjoy the taste and sensation of food—evolves as follows. The loss of an object, tangible or intangible, evokes a surge of oral instinctual impulses. The refusal to eat is at one and the same time an explicit denial that the oral instincts are on the ascendant *and* a defense against what (according to the conclusions of *infantile logic*) is the ego-threatening urge to incorporate and *merge*. The latter has been judged as dangerous and inimical to the continued existence of the ego. But the oral incorporative instincts are, as we well know, deeply imbedded in the total biophysiological structure of the individual and will not be denied! In simplest schematic form, the somatic and psychological symptoms of depression represent efforts to fill an insatiable appetite according to the *infantile mode*. They do so in such a way that the manifestations of the depression—i.e., the symptoms themselves—effectively disguise the hunger impulse that are the basis for the establishment of the symptomatology in the first place. Perhaps to some extent convulsive therapy is effective in depressive reactions in such dramatic fashion because, from the viewpoint of the depressed person's unconscious, the urge to *merge* is realized despite the defensive "posture" denying any such impulses. The seizure itself is most reminiscent of the *tremor response* already discussed, and the post-seizure sucking and mouthing behavior seems most suggestive to me.

The depressed person fills his emptiness with those sensory phenomena clinically identified as "symptoms." As we proceed to develop further the symbolic meaning of depressive symptomatology, we must consider the "loss" which is characteristic and universally present in depressive reactions. *Infantile logic* is based not only on the association of events but employs symbolism as well, as a step toward the representation of ideas and objects by words. Two events are equated in the symbolic system which infants develop, even if the only thing they hold in common is the quality of oppositeness. Any similarity, no matter how minute or trivial, is quite sufficient to justify their identity in the unconscious. In psychoanalytic writings the sexual symbolism with which various objects and circumstances may be endowed by the unconscious are well-known. Symbolic equations established in regard to orality are equally well-known.

When the *weaning process* undergoes distortion so that the *infantile mode* is put aside rather than being renounced as a way of life, the shift from breast or bottle to spoon and cup may be conceived of by the infant as the loss of an object precious to him. He may view the matter not as a major change towards the goal of maturity, but as a deprivation—a punishment, perhaps, for behavior which, according to the *infantile logic,* has been found responsible for withdrawal of the breast. As a matter of interest, in those instances of depression where the infantile origins can be scrutinized in some detail, it appears that there was *from the infant's point of view* the concept that the breast, once so freely given, was not relinquished by himself but taken away by his mother. The infant experiences no sense of accomplishment from this kind of "weaning." He has not resolved the dilemma of the *weaning process,* but is left with the impression that there was a deprivation for cause and that it only remains to discover the secret of how to recover in the present what he lost in the past. The object whose loss evoked the depressive reaction is specific in the sense that it has served as a substitute (transference) object for the filling breast of infancy. The subjective feelings of guilt and worthlessness have their nature predicated on the *infantile theory* that holds that he was weaned for "cause." Now when in adult life the individual suffers a "loss" of such special symbolic significance to his unconscious mind, this "loss" is immediately compared with and equated with the "loss" of the breast when the mother withdrew it years previously. Just as in that first instance where there was suffering which was utilized by the primitive ego to serve the function of filling the void resulting from the "loss," so there is a "replay" in the suffering and pain of depressive symptomatology of the drama of a portion of the *weaning process*. The symptoms of depression have physical concomitants because on the first occasion of the "loss" of an all-important object—the breast—the consequences were likewise physical discomfort.

In my clinical experience, patients with depressive symptoms often prove (when sufficient data is available) to have had mothers who acted upon unusually intense impulses to feed their children—not in the sense of providing food whenever the infant demanded it, but of "pushing" food on every possible occasion. These mothers are "food-oriented" and relate to their infants in large measure through this medium. They did not always overfeed in terms of calories, but their feeding efforts were unrelated to and independent of the infant's *hunger tide*. Reacting under the lash of the repetition compulsion, they continue this behavior all their lives, so that when one hears of the "feeding mother" who pushes unwanted food at times both related and unrelated to mealtime, one may be certain that the identical psychological position was ascribed to during the time she was taking care of her babies. Depressed people, in my experience, have been victims of

Theodore Lownik Library
109 Illinois Benedictine College
Lisle, Illinois 60532

prolonged and distorted nursing practices unrelated too often to sensations of hunger during their infancy. They are recruited from among those whose natural impulses toward achieving the *adult mode* were compromised by forcefully indulgent mothers.

The idea of depression must be distinguished from another clinical finding which it closely resembles and with which it is sometimes confused. "Apathy" is the consequence of never having had a suitable object to which the primitive ego could relate in the first place. It is an altogether different clinical state than depression, which comes as a consequence of a loss. It is typically seen in schizophrenia where, when associated with depression, it is most difficult to estimate the proportion of each.

CHAPTER VII

Nursing, Suicide, and Death

Contemplation of death, or suicidal thought, which amounts to the same thing, is a major preoccupation of mankind. It is a concern of religion, and though one may wish to avoid the idea, by the very nature of life one cannot. Death is very close to all of us, a relentless pursuer, the vision of which may be glorified but never ignored. Sometimes men seek death—or so it appears to the casual observer. Sometimes it seems in seeking death people hope to dominate it. At others there are quite rational reasons for finding the burdens of living outweighing the gratifications thereof. So suicide cannot, on the face of it alone, be considered pathological.

A consideration of this human concern about life, so often expressing itself as preoccupation with death, almost demands comment. This is not an appropriate place for more than a few passing comments on a most complex subject. As a psychiatrist I have had considerable experience with suicide over the years. Nor am I unaware that my conclusions differ from those of others, some of whom have had more day-to-day contact with the subject than I. But what follows is how I find and understand it.

"Suicide" is rarely successful! Those seemingly bent upon their own destruction may fail due to ineptness, or they may be frustrated in their efforts by the purposeful or accidental intervention of others. But true suicides, in contrast to pseudosuicides, usually see to it that if their first try fails, their further efforts toward self-destruction are successful. The true suicide, by definition, is one who has a preponderant desire to cease functioning as a human being. The pseudosuicide gives tongue and action to the idea, but his real intention is in the direction of living, not dying. If he dies he does so by misadventure, accident, or miscalculation. If the true suicide lives he does so for precisely the same reasons.

The isolated wish to die is a rarity. Only a small percentage, if any, of those who perish through conscious acts designed to "end it all" have such an intent dissociated from other considerations. Thus, from the very first, I want to emphasize that "suicide"—a term generally used to describe an act against the self ending in death—does not take into account the motive behind the act. The term is used both loosely and inaccurately by many lay and professional people, who mistakenly include in this term all self-perpetrated acts ending in one's own demise.

It is often assumed that because a man slashes his wrists with a razor blade or a woman swallows a handful of sleeping pills that his or her intent is to terminate life. The result does not necessarily reflect the motivation.

There is very little to be said about true suicides. They are generally successful and there is little opportunity to study their motivations. Speculations have been made that a considerable portion of accidental deaths are, in fact, suicides—an interesting thought, but so beyond our present capabilities of confirmation that one can go no further with the topic than to speculate upon it.

In contrast, pseudosuicides offer a great many opportunities for study. Not only do they provide abundant data, but they represent, as far as is presently known, the vast majority of "suicides." My definition for the term suicide emphasizes the unconscious motivation behind the behavior rather than what is consciously perceived to be the desired end result. It is well-known that most "suicidal" patients have unconscious motivations to be rescued by some other person. The flagrant appeal for "rescue" made by the individual who attains the heights of a bridge or window ledge and then threatens to jump is so obvious

112

that sometimes onlookers urge the person to make good his threat. They do not, of course, expect him to do so. They taunt him because his pretense is so apparent. Whether or not he jumps or permits himself to be rescued is not relevant to this particular study. What is of the greatest importance for our purpose is the question of what psychological motivation brought him to the emotional straits wherein he threatened "suicide." The wish to be "rescued" contains within it implications of far-reaching consequence. What is meant by "rescue" and how, in the suicide's mind, is "rescue" anticipated? What secret does the suicide keep even from himself when he avowedly attempts to "end it all?" Let us consider what happens when a "suicide" is rescued.

We observe, first of all, that the details of the circumstances suggest that a stage for the "suicide" has been unconsciously set in such a way that discovery by the intended rescuer is certain—or nearly so. To demonstrate with a clinical example: We learn that the patient has "tried suicide" on two occasions. In the first attempt she converted an angry husband into a rescuing one by taking a handful of sleeping pills before his very eyes. Her husband rushed her to the hospital where, with prompt medical treatment, her life was saved. On the second occasion when she became "upset" she began taking sleeping pills in close succession during the evening. Every time she arose from the stuporous state resulting from already ingested capsules, she took another dose. She did not tell her husband and he left for work in the morning unaware of what she had been doing. Actually her technique for "suicide" was almost guaranteed not to produce death! The most each additional capsule of sedative medication could produce would be sleep, which would mitigate against further drug incorporation. She was "rescued" by a neighbor who, coming to her house for an accustomed morning visit, found the patient sleeping in a chair at the

113

kitchen table, head pillowed on arms. The neighbor became frightened when she could not awaken the patient and called a physician.

The "rescuer," the reader observes, was no stranger, but one with whom the patient was on quite familiar terms and whose appearances at the patient's home were reasonably predictable. Having obtained certain gratifications in the past from the person chosen as "rescuer," the pseudo-suicide unconsciously manages to set the scene with sufficient subtlety to allay the "rescuer's" suspicions that the attempt might be ungenuine. He arranges to "commit suicide" in such a way that his plan will be foiled by the "rescuer." He makes an overt gesture, and the "rescuer"—if he plays the role "assigned" to him by the patient's unconscious—rushes the patient to a hospital emergency room where nurses cluster around ministering to the victim while a physician does what he can to restore what the patient has seemingly tried to destroy. Anyone who has observed the relationship which exists between "rescued" and "rescuer" may have observed the intensity and special quality of that relationship.

Not long ago I was asked to see in consultation a young man who had attempted "suicide" by slashing his wrists. When I came to the accident room to examine him I found him sitting up in bed, his wrists bandaged, and a rather attractive girl of his own age sitting at his bedside spooning food into his mouth. This was his girl friend—the "rescuer" whom he had called by phone after he had cut his wrists with a razor following a pique of anger at her "coldness." I held out a paper to be signed by him. He took it, reaching for it with his left hand. Grasping the pen I proffered in his right, he signed his name to the document without any difficulty. And all this while being fed by the girl, who behaved toward him as though they both believed he was helpless and had to be mothered! Her apparent assumption of guilt for what he had done, and his calm satisfaction in the way the affair had turned out, were palpable. They were displaying with unmasked abandon that special relationship which the young man's attempt on his own life had brought into exquisite focus.

The scene I have just described contains all of the factors necessary to understand the secret wish lurking behind every act of so-called "suicide." The person who wishes to "take his life" feels lonely, empty, depressed, or disappointed. Life, as he finds it at that moment, is not worth living. Something is lacking and he is certain, without really putting thought into words, that this emptiness need not be endured. He harbors the conviction that there is some "thing" somewhere which can relieve his loneliness. He cannot name it, nor even imagine what this "thing" might be. But he is absolutely certain that such an object exists! Moreover, he does not question the attainability of a state wherein he may be freed of those painful affects he currently suffers. The unverbalized idea becomes an unassailable article of faith. He does not demand to know what he seeks, but asks only "where is it?" There is a grain of historical truth in his idea that there is some "thing" which relieves. What his unconscious cannot grasp is that this "thing," though available at one time in his existence, is no longer attainable. He retains only the longing for it, and an unswerving certainty that if there was once a "thing" that relieved his discomfort, this is proof unto itself that "it" not only *still* exists, but can be called upon once again if only the exhortation to make it reappear can be discovered. (Reminiscent of the fairy tale of Aladdin's lamp, where by rubbing the lamp while intoning a magical formula, the genie is brought forth.) It hardly need be said that the sought-for "thing" *was* a reality in those halcyon times when sensations of hunger were abolished by nursing at breast or bottle.

But why should some people choose to compulsively carry out the charade of "suicide?" Surely there are less strenuous and certainly far less dangerous ways than self-destructive feints to ensure that one will be looked after and taken care of! There is, of course—save for the fact that none of the alternatives satisfies the compulsion to symbolically repeat in the present what has, in fact, been experienced in the past. Such individuals have had the misfortune of retaining elements of the *infantile mode*. In a word, they have not completed the *weaning process*. They have not totally relinquished the responses of the *infantile mode* and have adhered instead to unconscious patterns of reacting which should have been repressed.

This must not be naïvely considered to mean that the actual behavior of the early phases of the *weaning process* is displayed by such adults. I intend, rather, to convey the idea that the psychological position of the *infantile mode* is retained. The retention of this fixated position in the unconscious is what constitutes the predisposition to the development of pseudosuicide. It is always standing in the wings, waiting to be cued on stage. The psychodynamics can best be understood if one considers first of all that in such persons there has never been a "settlement" in regard to weaning. The *weaning process* has been completed per forma, but the idea has lingered in the unconscious that the breast is retrievable if only one invokes the proper magical rituals. It is a theory, so to speak, based on the conclusions achieved through the application of *infantile logic*, which has it that the breast was withdrawn because the behavior which had hitherto "caused" it to appear became no longer effective. The infant's "mind" is incapable of considering that the assumption upon which this "theory" was built may be invalid. The capability to question without prejudice that which one believes is a mark of advanced maturity. The infant's narcissism permits of no such challenges. The simplest conclusion, based on what the infant "knows," is that his behavior—which earlier brought forth this marvel—has somehow failed. The formula, or ritual, has somewhere not been followed—it being assumed all along that it is possible for the breast to be "recalled." That assumption is never questioned. The only problem remaining, according to the magical precepts believed to hold sway in infancy, is the rediscovery of the requisite incantation. (Reminiscent of the nursery stories featuring caves filled with treasure which will open if only one knows and intones the proper magical formula.)

I ask the reader to keep always in mind that what I write is "in a manner of speaking," and that the process is in actuality not carried out with verbal symbols.

The infant's next step is to try to rediscover the formula in whose existence and efficacy he has not the slightest doubt. We must now bring into juxtaposition with the above another association the infant made during the *weaning process*. We have learned how first *merging* and later *raptus* has been an integral part of the total psycho-physiological act of nursing. We have further come to understand that in the *weaning process* the conflict arising between the *infantile* and the *adult mode* of eating centers about this component. It follows then, according to the "laws" of *infantile logic*, that an associative connection is made between being *merged* and the act of suckling. That is to say, the infant comes to the conclusion that the behavior which brought forth the breast was the state of *merging* into which he passed while nursing. In brief, he takes it that he got the breast because he *merged*. Now while *merging* is permissible enough when the ego is not yet well-organized, it is prohibited to the more mature ego because the *merged* state is experienced as inimical to the continued existence of the ego itself.

Thus, for those who later in life become depressed there remains an unresolved conflict, banished, for the most part, to the unconscious mind where it is partly hidden from view. The "loss" preceding the onset of depressive symptoms rekindles the previously repressed conflict. The idea that relief can be called forth—that there is "something" which will cure—gains the ascendant at the same time that the ego retreats to boundaries more appropriate to an earlier age. The individual having become "emptied" as it were, because of the devastation he experiences from the loss he has endured, seeks to ameliorate matters by "filling" the void thus perceived. No present reality or object relationship adequately serves such a purpose for his unconscious. That is why the depressed are universally pessimistic about ever attaining their former level of satisfaction. There is but one object which, in the depressed one's unconscious, will satisfactorily fill the void consequent to the precipitant "loss." The unresolved conflicts generated during the *weaning process* break out of the bounds previously restraining them. Once again the conflicting forces are experienced. The urge to *merge* is confronted by its opposition, the fear of ego loss.

It is reasonable to assume that an infant sometimes comes to the erroneous conclusion that *because* he *merges* he is fed. Some infants, according to this view, come to comprehend the events of the *weaning process* in a different way than is generally the case. This idea that the *merging causes* the breast to be presented to him is not arbitrary. There are, in the infantile experience of those destined to become depressed in later life, events which are entirely compatible with this particular distortion of the associational connections. If, for example, during infancy the feedings are administered not according to the needs of the infant, but primarily at the convenience of the mother or in consonance with her compulsive needs to be a "good mother," such a distortion can readily occur. For when the infant is offered milk while in a state of satiation— when he is not really hungry—then he might very well come to the conclusion that there is no particularly important relationship between crying and being hungry and being nursed. But because it is associated with *merging,* it would under such circumstances, be rather likely that the association of merging = feeding be more firmly established than the association of hunger = feeding.

Does the wish to die implicit in the idea of self-destruction represent desire to relinquish existence forever? The

118

fact of death, even when avowedly thought to be a final "nothingness," can in fact never really be grasped by the human mind. It is beyond our real experience. We compare it with what we have known. We cannot exceed the boundaries of our own experience in our efforts to understand it.

In a certain sense the *merging* response constitutes a "death." It seems to me that when one comes to contemplate the idea of one's personal demise that one retrieves the nonverbal memory traces relating to the first "brush with death"—*merging*. As in death, there is a dissolution of the ego when one *"merges,"* whether at the breast during infancy or during genital sexual relations at the moment of orgasm. Thus, the apparent seeking for "death" of the person bent on "ending it all" seems to be not a search for death as such—i.e., a permanent state of nothingness—but rather a springboard to a way of living more gratifying than the present one.

Ideas of resurrection and, more especially, immortality are strong within the minds of would-be suicides. Sometimes one uncovers the most remarkable convictions of invulnerability. A first try of suicide is followed by a second and a third because with each survival the belief in personal indestructibility is merely strengthened. I don't believe I have ever examined a "suicide" who really grasped the full extent of the danger to which he had exposed himself. Even nurses and physicians who tried suicide have seemed to put their professional knowledge aside and have not fully assessed the risks to which they have exposed themselves. All have treated their "suicidal" actions actions as trivial and unimportant. They have assumed the attitude, "It really couldn't have been as dangerous as the doctor claims or else I should not still be alive!"

One must keep in mind that no matter how intense the belief in the absence of an afterlife, no matter how intelligent the person or how devoted he is to the idea that death is the "end," all men harbor within themselves—

whether or not they are aware of it—an equal certainty that the infinitude of death cannot be so. We need to keep constantly in mind that man has no way of knowing death. We rely for what knowledge we have of the subject on experiences we take to be akin to death. Sleep, for example, is commonly equated with death. Perhaps such comparison is derived—aside from the apparent similarity—from a deep longing within us all that death be as impermanent a state as sleep. It will be recalled that *merging* is renounced as a way of life during the *weaning process* because of the fear of the loss of ego boundaries. In contrast, sleep results from the ego's willing relinquishment of object relationships —a far different thing, the reader will appreciate, than the experience of ego *loss* during the *weaning process.*

The depressed person has, of course, given up the manifestations of *merging*, but he retains a remnant desire— unbeknownst to himself—to return to what is "remembered" as that blissful state of oblivion enjoyed at the mother's breast known as *merging.* So when suicide is contemplated, or the idea of dying is acted upon, death is but the manifest wish, containing within it the latent wish to *merge* once again at the mother's breast—if at the same time we review our understanding that an intimate association between *merging* and nursing exists in the mind from the time of infancy: that to *merge* is equated with the incorporation of milk. And, of course, suckling at the breast being the earliest means by which the empty feelings of hunger could be replaced by a sensation of satiation, the nursing situation becomes the prototype solution to the problem evoked by the experience of all future "emptinesses" of any kind whatever. By such reasoning, then, we come to the conclusion—borne out, in my judgment, by the clinical fact that most suicides survive their attempts— that it is not death which is sought, but rather life. A fresh start, beginning where the awareness of one's life begins in the first place, seems to be the unconscious desire that motivates the behavior. The rescuer symbolically serves in the present the function of the mother during infancy. Moreover, an identical search for that which can never be recovered can be recognized as a fundamental motivation for the concern and preoccupation with death cited earlier. Death is equated in the unconscious with that experience seemingly equivalent with it—*merging*, which is feared but desired as well. The idea that man could desire the void of death clashes discordantly with what we know of nature's determination to preserve, promote, and maintain life against all odds. Just as the manifest dream content must be reduced to its latent meaning to be really understood, so must a desire for one's own demise be analyzed and its latent meaning extracted before such a "death wish" can be understood.

CHAPTER VIII

Ego Immaturity: Homosexuality

It is fair to say, I think, that there is a great deal of misinformation, confusion, and misapprehension about the topic of homosexuality. All sorts of "causes" have been offered in explanation of the phenomenon, but an all-encompassing theory for homosexuality has not, in my opinion, been developed. Psychoanalytic explanation has come closest to the mark, I think, but falls somewhat short of throwing full light on the overall phenomenology. Perhaps the present unsatisfactory state of our understanding is related to the fact that the symbolic meaning of homosexual behavior and ideation has been too often overlooked. It is often treated as though it were explanatory unto itself and that the details of homosexuality are to be interpreted literally rather than figuratively. It occurs to me that progress might be made if homosexuality is considered analogous to the manifest content of a dream. Perhaps the analysis of the latent content will, as in the case of dreams, reveal an otherwise unrecognized meaning to the behavior.

The technique Freud employed with such brilliant success in bringing to light the latent meaning of manifest dream content is applicable to the other manifestations of mental activity. At least there seems no valid objection to approaching the problem of homosexuality from that point of view. Therefore, just as one does not consider that the manifest content of a dream represents its actual meaning, so one should recognize that a study of homosexual behavior without reference to the latent meanings thereof may fill out some of the details in already charted areas, but is unlikely to suggest a fresh point of view.

Whether confined to fantasy or displayed in overt behavior, "homosexual" urges have identical origins in the psyche. It is to the identification and explanation of these psychological origins that this chapter is directed.

Homosexual men—that is, men who lead the "gay life" —have a saying: "Today's queen is next year's trade." Translated into idiomatic English, this means that he who employs his sexual organ to penetrate one of the body orifices of another man subsequently seeks gratification by himself being penetrated by another. In "homosexual" practices the urge to be penetrated predominates over the desire to penetrate. What it all comes down to is that in homosexuality the gratification from sucking turns out to be more satisfying than the pleasure of orgasm. Translated into everyday language, this truism says that even though a homosexual may commence his perverse sexual practices by having partners perform fellatio on him, he sooner or later seeks his pleasure by performing fellatio on other men. Let me now put the same finding into a frame of reference where the anatomical relationship established between homosexual partners is stressed.

I have not found the various current classifications of "homosexuality" very useful as an aid to understanding the psychodynamics of this behavior. Nor do any of these classifications conveniently lend themselves to presentation of the subject in the particular way necessary to demonstrate the relationship between "homosexuality" and events of the *weaning process*. I have, for this reason, devised a nomenclature which approaches the subject from this particular point of view. I classify "homosexuality" according to the function a portion of the anatomy of each partner performs. The simplest imaginable scheme is thereby proposed which has, at the same time, applicability to overt behavior as well as to fantasies of physical relationship with homosexual partners. Furthermore, classifying homosexual relationships according to functional considerations obviates the need to postulate a separate theory to explain lesbianism. In effect, I have deemphasized the sexual elements in "homosexuality" and have centered attention on the function performed in the psyche for whatever juxtaposition of body parts may be involved. In some important regards the term "homosexuality" is misleading, for it designates as "sexual" a range of phenomena that are only superficially so. In my opinion a more accurate term might be "homo-pseudosexuality."

The detail of homosexual activity or fantasy provides the criteria whereby a participant may be classfied as belonging to one and occasionally both of the following categories:

1. *The Penetrator Homosexual*: One who penetrates with some portion of his or her anatomy the body orifices or folds of a partner of the same sex with the conscious aim of achieving libidinal gratification.

2. *The Receptor Homosexual*: One who takes into the folds or the body orifices some part of the anatomy of a partner of the same sex with the conscious aim of achieving libidinal gratification.

This classificatory arrangement defines the relationship not in terms of specific anatomic organs, but rather in terms of the functional relationship which comes into being when there is physical contact between partners. My emphasis on the penetrator and recepter functions of physical juxtaposition assists in developing the thesis that "homosexuality" originates from unresolved conflicts established far earlier in life than the term "homosexuality" implies. To this point no mention has been made of the emotional aspects of the "homosexual" relationship. The infantile quality of this is well known. One of my patients suggested the following equation: Homosexuality is to heterosexuality as masturbation is to intercourse with the woman you love.

The first case I offer in illustration is that of a 23-year-old man of better-than-average intelligence. He was initiated into "homosexual" practices when, at the age of 8, an older boy "forced" him to perform fellatio. He found

124

the activity very exciting, and this relationship continued without substantial change until he was twenty. His friend, to employ now my nomenclature, was the *penetrator;* he was the *receptor.* Sometimes intercrural intercourse was performed upon him and once or twice he was the *receptor* in anal intercourse. There were, in addition to this first partner, several others, but he did not display the florid promiscuousness that is so frequently associated with those who practice "homosexuality"—the constant search for an elusive "something," the discovery of which seems ever within one's grasp but somehow always out of reach. My patient's gratification in the physical relationship with his friend was twofold. First, and consciously the more important, was the pleasure he took in evoking excitation in the *penetrator, i.e.,* in causing the *penetrator* to perform his assigned role. The second satisfaction was accomplished by the "mouthing" maneuvers (this term was his own) which he carried out once his oral cavity had been penetrated. The very thought of semen entering his mouth produced feelings of nausea, and on the one and only occasion when this occurred he reacted by becoming "deathly ill" and retching for a considerable but undetermined period of time. During the "mouthing" (which on further examination proved to be identical with sucking) his major endeavor was to achieve a psychological state of "being out of it." This sought-for state was, as far as I could tell from his description, identical with the *merging* response. There was no verbal content—no images or fantasies which he could recall having had on these occasions.

At the time he began psychotherapy he was living with his mother. Shortly before his father had died. During the preceding several years his older siblings had gone on their own one by one until he was the only child remaining at home. For years he had felt strongly attracted to the priesthood, and shortly after his father's death had renounced his perverse practices in anticipation of becoming a member of the clergy. Shortly after he had made these decisions, however, he began to experience increasingly severe attacks of anxiety when he attended mass. These attacks were triggered when, during the ceremony, the celebrant elevated the Host, presenting it for veneration by the assembled congregation. He had always cultivated intense relationships with priests and was adept at maneuvering them in various ways, the accomplishment of which gave him feelings of great inner satisfaction. He would secretly and privately gloat over the subtle control he exercised, or felt he exercised over them. Just before he came for therapy he had become increasingly anxious in the presence of one particular priest with whom he had a close relationship, maintained in large measure by deep and prolonged discussion of the patient's feelings, especially those of a religious nature.

The patient had, since the beginning of his aberrant sexual behavior, kept his perverse practices very much a secret. To the world he presented the picture of a nice, pleasant, inoffensive young man who was always ready to listen to the problems of others and to be of help wherever he could. The central figure of his life was his mother. His father had been away from home during his childhood and youth, and nothing more intimate than a formal father-son relationship had developed between them. He had a rather cold, somewhat disdainful attitude toward his siblings, whom he considered as annoyances who had always interfered with the attachment between his mother and himself. He never accorded them the position of real people. This feeling, as far as I could tell, was reciprocated by them.

His childhood was charactertized by a special feature I find of great significance. At the age of six he began to gain weight. Over the next several years he became grossly obese and was unable, on this account, to participate in school athletics as he wished. At about the age of 13, because his physical appearance caused him embarrassment, he tried to limit his food intake so as to lose weight. But his mother scuttled this ambition of his with skill and precision. She actively discouraged him from his resolve, tempting him beyond his capacity to resist with especially delicious deserts which she would encourage him to eat with such words as "One little desert isn't going to hurt you now!" In retrospect, however, one could discover the reason for the patient's obedient concurrence with his mother's desire that he remain "fat." There was, so to speak, an active conspiracy between them to undermine his resolve. His mother was one of those women for whom the label "feeder" seems quite apropos— a woman always pushing food at others and forever getting "hurt" when her offer is not accepted and consumed.

At age 18 he again tried to limit his caloric intake. This time he succeeded in reducing his weight to the normal figure he has since maintained. Perhaps a growing maturity finally made it possible for him to resist more successfully on this occasion the seductive offerings of food by his mother. Her constant pressures on him to take food from her did not abate. She simply ignored his avowed desire to attain an average weight.

There are, of course, further details of his behavior and fantasy life which have much of significance to contribute to our understanding of the psychodynamics of his "homosexuality." He would purchase what he called "muscle books"—magazines featuring photographs of men so posed as to display their muscular development. He would choose from whatever selection was available in one of these periodicals the picture which most appealed to him. He would then place this picture in a position where he could conveniently inspect it and, gazing at it with a look that he described as having an "unusual quality," would masturbate. He would always select a specific portion of the subject's anatomy on which to concentrate his attention— namely, the bulge produced by contraction of the pectoral muscles! He indicated, further, how important a feature the pectoral musculature was for him by relating that he went to special pains to find those pictures which seemed to focus attention upon the pectorales. For these were the pictures which he found most exciting and the ones which, in his own words, "turned me on." There was no articulate fantasy accompanying his masturbation, but he did tell me that on these occasions he would "lose myself." One piece of behavior accompanying his masturbation seems to me especially significant. He would gaze at the curve of one of his own breasts, maneuvering his body and tensing his muscles to make this portion of his anatomy as large and rounded as possible. While maintaining this posture he would then carry masturbation to its climactic conclusion. He went on to say that while masturbating he would find himself "holding my mouth in some kind of certain way"—a posture which enhanced the *merging* sensation which he sought at the moment of climax.

His relationships with girls are customarily platonic. But with one he has "made out" on a few occasions. His girl friend is obviously quite fond of him and I think in many ways a little reminiscent of his mother in view of her easily evoked manipulative behavior. She does not object to having sexual relations. However, she clings to religious principles she would prefer adhering to were it possible to do so without risking loss of his interest. She has let him know she would prefer preserving her virginity until marriage. This attitude, of course, fits in marvelously with this young man's obvious heterosexual reticence. He reveals, in this connection, that he has been hesitant to make sexual advances, and more especially has avoided touching her breasts despite the "temptation" he has experienced to do so. On one occasion when they were "necking" he was aware that she turned her body in such manner that his hand, without any initiation of his own, came to rest directly upon her breast. At this turn of events he studiously avoided making the slightest movement of his fingers. He said he felt no desire to do so though he was, the the time of my interview, aware of a curious feeling within himself—somehow connected with this experience—which, however, he could not further describe. He knows that other men experience the urge to fondle, and his own inhibition in this area he finds disheartening.

On one occasion he related his feelings in reflecting upon the opinion of an acquaintance that "happiness is a tit full of whiskey." "You know, doctor," he confided, "if I ever sucked a breast I'd crack up." He deftly encourages his girl friend to assume an aggressive role in their love making. He is pliable in her hands, to a purpose, and his initiative is severely impaired. When they kiss he waits in hope that she will penetrate his mouth with her tongue. He never experiences erection during this lovemaking. Indeed, genital aims are notably absent, and though the physical aspects of the relationship have what one would have to agree is a sexual coloring, his aim is oral—in a specific passive-receptive way. His psychosexual development has been arrested and is fixated at an oral level. He is the *receptor* in a far larger sense than the limitations imposed by the term in my classification of "homosexuality." His whole attitude and position in life is that of being a "receiver," a role he assiduously cultivates. He uses his eyes in a manner which is of considerable interests in view of the transition that is normally made from *merging* to *raptus*. He frequently indulges in raptus, staring at some object without concentrating on it, all the while holding his mouth open. He has, in the past, experienced a great deal of satisfaction from catching another person's glance and then "staring him down." He found the experience exhilarating because it appealed to him as a danger of some kind. On occasion during his therapeutic sessions he reported blocking out the meaning of what I might say and instead indulging in a sense of gratification he had come to experience by listening to the sound of my voice. He would, at such times, assume an open-mouthed posture while staring off into space.

What can one make of this data? That the young man is seriously disturbed there can be no doubt. By definition he is a *receptor* of many stimuli. His receptor activity in homosexual relationships tends to divert attention from the importantt fact that his sexual behavior is but one segment of his total behavior. And this total behavior is directed toward the taking in of stimuli through "all channels." And, when we recognize that sexuality is not the core of his existence and is more determined by oral factors than itself setting the tone of the character, we understand that he would be no less psychologically impaired—indeed, there would have been no psychodynamic difference of any significance—had there been no overt *receptor* homosexual behavior at all. To him the penis served as an acceptable object for oral gratification, one with which he could *merge* without experiencing the fear engendered when, as an infant, he *merged* with the breast. What he found attractive in men were the bulges and rounded parts of their bodies. Thin men held no attraction whatever. So it was not *men,* in terms of sexuality, to whom he turned, but rather persons with rounded parts, reminiscent of the breast but which at the same time were as far removed from that organ in actuality as his unconscious could manage. The "rounded parts" of women were much too closely associated with the fear he experienced in relationship with the original object of his oral impulses. His *raptus* behavior in regard to his own breast tells us in a quite specific way what had all along been the object of his oral impulses. The reasonings of *infantile logic* result in the equation of rounded objects with the first recognizable outside object—the mother's breast. Whether his masturbatory fantasy took for its object a woman's breast, or his own, or some symbolic representation thereof, the most impressive element is that the core of his libidinal desire was oral in origin. His own breast is specifically chosen as a substitute for the maternal breast because it is not dangerously reminiscent of it. On the other side of the coin, his disinterest in having contact with *any* female breast is but a defense against the intense fear the idea of "breast" evokes in his unconscious—a fear of such massive proportions because of the long, lingering "dangerous" wish to *merge* with it as he once did.

I have chosen this case because a good deal is known about the characteristics of the patient's mother's personality and her way with him when he was an infant. He was actually breast fed for nine months. She seems to have had a great personal need to demonstrate her motherliness. She appears to have forced herself on her youngest son, a piece of behavior especially believable in view of the remote relationship her alcoholic husband maintained with her. He drank rather heavily and was away from the home a good deal of the time. I rather think she exploited the dependency of the patient during his early months and in so doing convinced him that the receptor position, psychologically speaking, was the only one to assume if he was to stay in her good graces.

The reader understands, of course, that behavior in the present is very often a kind of "replay" of earlier experiences, the present and past having symbolic equivalence despite the manifest differences between them. Thus, when we learn that his mother pushes food at him to this very day and that he has to "get really mad" to cause her to desist, we do not have to strain our imaginations to recognize that this behavior has been characteristic of her all along. Indeed, we know this almost as a certainty because of the patient's earlier period of obesity and his mother's not-so-subtle objections to his wish to bring his body proportions closer to normal. His mother liked his obesity, doubtless for more than one reason, but probably a powerful motivation was her desire to have a constant reminder that she was, indeed, a successful feeder.

But can we, from this, formulate an explanation for the particular path the patient's psychological development followed? The best we can do is offer the plausible because, as has been pointed out, certain knowledge of what transpires within the psyche of the preverbal infant is not obtainable. Plausible and probable information is possible, for earlier events give rise to behavioral and attitudinal manifestations later in life, which when subjected to critical analysis yield the probable circumstances of their origins.

During his *weaning process* the patient had displayed manifestations of preverbal psychic conflict. These were engendered as his developing ego became aware of its "annihilation" each time he *merged* with the breast he suckled. But as his strivings toward the *adult mode* proceeded, *raptus* gradually replaced *merging*. His natural inclination was to proceed to the *adult mode* of eating, but his mother misinterpreted the manifestations of conflict (identical with the nine-month anxiety of Redlich), and when he refused to suckle redoubled her efforts to nurse him. An infant has no choice but to swallow when his oral cavity is flooded with liquid milk which flows freely from a lactating breast. And the hierarchy of reflexes is so arranged that swallowing occurs before inhalation of liquid can take place. Thus, though his ego had determined not to suckle milk out of fear of *merging* he had, in fact, no choice in the matter. His wishes, being unrecognized and unappreciated, were simply overcome by his overzealous mother. He met what might be called the "nutritional assault" of his mother by assuming a *receptor* position in relationship to her. He would take milk if it were pushed at him, but he would exercise no effort on his own part to obtain it. By exchanging passive reception for active acquisitive behavior he avoided the responsibility for the "perils" of *merging* with the breast. At least this seems to have been the conclusion resulting from the application of *infantile logic* to the solution of a troublesome problem. But in the meantime he continued to have *merging* experiences at a time when his ego, still extending its bounderies, grasped a new idea, namely, that *merging,* frightening and dangerous when achieved by active suckling at the breast, could be experienced by having it forced upon one. In a certain sense, because of his particular nursing situation, he learned too early that *merging* was not, as it had at first seemed, dangerous and an experience to be avoided and renounced. Furthermore, this maternal interference with the natural and normal sequences of the *weaning process* meant that *merging* derivatives became an integral part of his adult behavior. There was, consequently, no shift from oral to genital *merging* as a desired and valued experience, which normally takes place. Instead of a shift from the oral to the genital executive of *merging,* only a partial object change was accomplished. The aim to *merge* remained constant, but the aim shifted from the breast itself to objects symbolically equated therewith.

The anxiety or the defenses against it (apathy, disinterest, repulsion, etc.) evoked in "homosexuals" indicates a reaction formation. Only the object of the oral impulse is modified. The aim to incorporate and *merge* remains unchanged. Where the *adult mode* holds sway, *both* aim and object change. The mark of the retention of the *infantile mode* is the pseudoshift of object without change of the oral incorporative libidinal aim. This young man's sexual activity has always served his more primitive oral wishes and has, in fact, never been sexual at all if the psychological mechanisms of his behavior be the item by which the matter can be judged. We are more interested in coming to understand the basic conflicts exemplified in this condition than with emphasizing the "sexual" aspects. We have adequate reason to believe, I think, that the cloak of sexuality has been employed as a defense against recognition of the long forbidden but not renounced oral receptive wish to suckle and *merge.* Thus, we come to recognize that "homosexuality," in this one case at least, has at its core oral conflicts finding expression in behavior easily misjudged as fundamentally "sexual" in nature.

Clinical material from a second case follows, which in my judgment supports the concept of "homopseudosexuality." Disguised behind the *receptor homosexual's* activity lurks the instinctual urge to suckle. The one object with which a relationship is usually avoided and feared by the *receptor homosexual* is the female breast. This attitude is an example, I think, wherein the unconscious wish is discoverable in the excessiveness of the protest. For the *receptor homosexual* the object of his unmodified instinctual impulse is as far removed from (and simultaneously as reminiscent of) the mother and the mother's breast as possible. The instinctual urge to suckle according to the *infantile mode* remains unaltered. The path of discharge is achieved through a shift of the object of the instinctual suckling impulse to one sufficiently disguised to "fool" the ego. An object shift occurs out of the inner necessity to disguise the identity of the original object, yet is so chosen as to maintain the associations formed in relationship with the breast. It must be remembered that normally a complete shift from the first object of the oral incorporative aim takes place early in life, where the original object is replaced by a substitute rather than being renounced. By such a psychological maneuver the penis is substituted for the breast as the object of the unmodified infantile incorporative impulse. Such associations are customarily of the simplest kind, depending as they do on comparisons hardly comprehensible to those unfamiliar with unconscious mechanisms. For example, there follows the probable sequence of associations leading to such a conclusion via *infantile logic*.

A woman has something that "sticks out" from her body. So does a man. Therefore, the "reasoning" goes, both possess the same thing. The presence of erectile tissue in erotogenic organs are likewise sources of associations leading to the well-known symbolic equation: penis = breast. An adult would hardly confuse a dog with a cat but, because both have four legs, a small child may recognize no difference between them. Differences are less favored for comparison than similarities. Cows and bulls are all "cows" to small children. The differences so significant to adults in determining what distinguishes the one from the other, hold small significance for the child compared with what, to his way of thinking, is the identity of the form of one to that of the other.

Fellatio or cunnilinctus is the principle physical act performed in "homosexual" relationships. What the *receptor homosexual* does not consciously know is that his "sexual" behavior "replays" nursing scenes from his infancy. In my judgment, the evidence points to a fixation at a preverbal oral incorporative level; specifically to a failure to shift completely from the *infantile mode* to the *adult mode*. But what about *the penetrator homosexual?* There is nothing incorporative, as far as one can tell, in the observable portion of his "sexual" behavior. We have long ago learned, of course, that behavior may have much more to it than appears on the face of it. In the search for insight into the psychodynamics of behavior we always bear in mind the well-established principle that behind the manifest there resides the latent. By applying this principle to the consideration of the psychodynamic problem presented by the *penetrator homosexual* we come to understand the truth expressed by the truism quoted at the beginning of this chapter. That was, it will be recalled, a statement current in "homosexual" circles to the effect that with the passage of time those who are *penetrator homosexuals* become *receptor homosexuals*. In brief, that the universal denominator of "homosexuality" is *receptor homosexuality*. But this still does not answer the question of the psychodynamic forces motivating *penetrator* homosexuality. Why, if the conclusion I have drawn is true, should there be *penetrator homosexuals* at all? Why should a *penetrator* position be assumed at first and only after a time evolve into a *receptor* position? I think the explanation is to be found in the nature of the psychological defenses erected by the *penetrator homosexuals,* defenses which appear to serve the denial of *receptor wishes.* If it were otherwise, it would not be possible to explain the observed fact that "today's queen is next year's trade." I think the selection of the term "queen" for a *penetrator homosexual* speaks for itself. Nor must it be thought that the apparent shift from *penetrator homosexuality* to *receptor homosexuality* is as readily accomplished in an opposite direction. The shift in predilection from one type of "sexual" behavior to another is almost invariably in the direction indicated. The *penetrator homosexual* becomes the *receptor* in the same way, figuratively speaking, that "water seeks its own level." If we peer beneath the surface manifestations of his role in the physical relationship between "homosexuals" and consider the fantasies the *penetrator homosexual* entertains during his act of penetration, we'll discover that he identifies with the *receptor.* In other words, though he acts as the "penetrator" he obtains his satisfaction not with fantasies or thoughts connected with penetration of the body of another, but rather with speculations as to how it might be to be the *receptor.* His particular preoccupation is with the vicarious gratification he obtains through the behavior of his partner. This fantasy, this preoccupation with how it might feel to be the *receptor,* is by no means confined to "homosexual relationships." It is commonly found in men who, to all appearances, are "heterosexual." In heterosexual intercourse they sometimes wonder to themselves how it would "feel" from the woman's position, in pursuit of which they may question her as to what she experiences. It is not just manifest behavior which is important. Indeed, fantasies accompanying behavior, when it comes to the elucidation of psychodynamics, are much more important. A mature man, for example, does not wonder during intercourse how it might feel to be a woman! He is, instead, entirely taken up with the joy and satisfaction of being what in fact he is—a male, free to behave as such with as much vigor as nature has endowed him.

The next patient never considered himself "homosexual." From his point of view homosexuality was entirely of the "receptor" variety. He was married and though he was frigid (he never experienced *merging* during orgasm) to all other appearances his heterosexual life was not particularly remarkable.

Shortly after beginning therapy he dreamt that he was sucking an extraordinarily long and large penis. The dream ended in his having an orgasm. On several occasions in the past he had been the *penetrator* in relationships with other men. He enjoyed this acivity, finding it more satisfying than either normal heterosexual relationships or the experience of fellatio performed by a woman. "I've performed homo acts on my wife, too," he told me.

This man's mother was overly concerned with feeding him during infancy. She has told him many times that she breast fed him until he was nine months old and only gave it up then because her milk supply was outpaced by his demands. It was ascertained that he never experienced *merging* during sexual relations of any variety. Where in real life he has performed as the *penetrator*, part of his gratification was obtained through his unconscious identification with the *receptor*. It was for this reason that the satisfaction he experienced in having fellatio performed by a man so greatly exceeded the same experience with a female partner. The performance of one partner does not differ from that of the other. The difference lies in his identifying himself with a male who sucks, an identification fraught with anxiety where the partner was female. In the dream it was he who was the *receptor*. Curiously, his own genital is not brought into the manifest dream content. How could he experience orgasm when the dream represents that the penis belongs to another? And why is the penis represented as being so "long and large?" In the dream he was "curled up," he says on inquiry, a piece of

137

information that puts us in mind of the posture of a nursing infant. On the surface such a dream is a blatantly obvious one. It says "I perform fellatio." But at a more fundamental level the idea of being a *receptor* is presented: "I wish to suckle *and merge.*" This seems to be the explanation for the fact that when in the dream he is engaged in suckling activity, he experiences orgasm. It is not, it must be emphasized, a genital experience. In the dream he is curled up and sucking a large object. This is the manifest content of the dream and we must look under the surface to discover the latent one. His mouth is where the stimulus impinges. Hence, in my judgment this is an oral experience—a replay of the disguised and now forbidden suckling of the maternal breast. The syntax, so to speak, is homosexual—a presentation which disguises the underlying unconscious wish to replay the sucking gratifications of infancy. The emphasis on size certainly speaks for a time of life when such characteristics were more than trivial. The patient's inner confusion regarding anatomical differences between the sexes is hinted at by his comment about "homo" relationships with his wife, which is further support for his interpretation that breast = penis—a familiar enough equation.

This man, in another connection, relates that he has always done as others have felt was best for him. This particular character trait can best be explained, I think, by considering that during his *weaning process* he formed the infantile theory that he was nursed *because* he was compliant to his mother's demands. In adult terms this is to say, "You get along best when you do what others want you to do."

Returning to our study of his behavior we learn a fact that fits in very well with this conception. In his *penetrator homosexual* activity another man always requested permission to perform fellatio on him. He recalled occasions when he hoped that others would importune him to be a penetrator. In other words, the entire matter of his "homosexual" behavior was set up so that he acceded to a "demand" made upon him by another. It is not he who wishes to suckle, this seems to say, it is rather that others wish him to be the recipient of sensations which their sucking behavior provides. In my opinion, the overconcern of the patient's mother with his nursing was of great and crucial importance in the shaping of his character. He is unfortunate that his *weaning process* was not carried to a successful conclusion during his infancy. I think his mother probably fed him so assiduously because of her need to be what she considered a "good mother." She paid little attention to what he desired for himself, and from what I have observed elsewhere I imagine she refused to acknowledge his rebellion at being nursed when this event occurred during the *weaning process* because her own need to be the mother exceeded her desire to see him achieve the *adult mode*.

Nor should it be surprising that the same theme of being a *receptor* is found in other areas of his life. Before treatment he was a heavy beer drinker. Early in his career he would sip the brew slowly, but with the passage of time he would drink it in larger and larger gulps. Sometimes, he said, he would consume an entire bottle of beer with only two swallows. He described himself as a compulsive drinker. But it was only under circumstances of loneliness or boredom or inactivity that he felt so driven. Beer appealed to him because of the large volume he enjoyed swallowing. The other kinds of alcoholic beverages rarely were touched.

Overt "homosexuality" is, for reasons not sufficiently known, more frequent among males than females. Nonetheless, what holds in the case of one sex seems equally true in the other. The classificatory scheme of "*receptor homosexual*" and "*penetrator homosexual*" is just as useful in discussing female "homosexuality" as it has proven to be in the male. And, as occurs not infrequently in male "homosexuality," both "*penetrator homosexuality*" and "*re-*

139

ceptor homosexuality" can be found in the same individual. The following clinical case material will, I think, prove instructive.

The patient is a 40-year-old school teacher who comes for therapy because she desires help in terminating a "homosexual" relationship of some six years duration. She met her partner while the latter was a student teacher. A feeling of closeness developed between the two, although the value of it seemed far more important to my patient than to her partner.

The patient was married at the time this liaison began. Her husband was an overly accommodating person. If she showed no more than casual interest in some piece of furniture, jewelry, or item of clothing, he would go to unbelievable lengths to obtain the admired object for her. He was delighted when she found a friend in this student teacher. Learning from his wife that this girl had some sort of difficulty "back home," the husband suggested to the wife that the girl be invited to live with them. He expressed his thought that if she were troubled, perhaps living in a family setting would be of greater help to her than staying in the women's residence where she resided. Accordingly, the student teacher moved into the home with the patient and her husband.

No sooner had the younger woman come into the home than the patient's husband ceased sleeping with his wife, persuading her to take the younger woman as her bed partner! Why the husband pushed his wife towards this relationship is not certain. Perhaps his doing so was dictated by a need to please his wife or, what seems far more likely, by psychopathological elements beyond our knowledge. It seems likely that he, who was so attentive to her every material wish, was no less perspicacious when it came to his wife's libidinal interests. He was, as far as my patient knew, unaware of the physical relationship between herself and the student teacher. If one credits what he is reported to have said, his suggestion (that his wife sleep

140

with their guest) was intended to be therapeutic for the younger woman. He said he thought this would help the younger woman's "nervousness."

The younger woman, called "Moll," is described by the patient as physically strong and athletically inclined. Characterwise, "Moll" appears to be a pathological liar, offering falsehoods to the patient when the truth might serve her better. Prevarication is a way of life with her, consequently nothing about her can be relied upon. The patient has tried to behave in such ways that her friend would become more reliable and her behavior more predictable. But she has never discovered the formula she assumes exists which would enable her to bend "Moll" to her will.

"Moll" is a very flighty individual. She has other women besides the patient, and sometimes flaunts her relationships with them, or alternatively makes wild accusations that it is the patient who has been the unfaithful one. She disappears for weeks at a time and the patient suffers loneliness and longs for her return. Or, "Moll" will make a "date" and then not keep it. She will agree to talk by phone at a designated time and then renege. The patient becomes apprehensive at this. Perhaps, her thought goes, "Moll" will never return. The patient calls her friend on the phone, but "Moll" will not answer. This is especially disturbing to the patient when the latter knows for a certainty that "Moll" is home. This unresponsiveness on "Moll's" part causes the patient to go through agonies of anxiety. She paces about her home, walking aimlessly from room to room, saying to herself, "I won't survive without her, I won't survive without her."

On the physical side of the relationship "Moll" seemed to be the aggressive member of the partnership and the patient the passive, acquiescing one. That is to say, "Moll" made the first move" and used her mouth to kiss and suck the patient's lips, breasts and vulva "quite vigorously." Occasionally the patient would perform cunnilinctus, but

141

her greatest pleasure was experienced as a consequence of the mouthing by her partner. But, as before, if we study the fantasy in the patient at the time of the physical contact with her partner, we will come to a far deeper appreciation of the psychological meaning behind the apparent "homosexual" behavior. The patient fantasied doing as "Moll" did! She got vicarious gratification from what oral pleasures she imagined "Moll" got while the latter was sucking. The patient related that her own satisfaction was obtained not in having portions of her body sucked upon, but from imagining how it must be at such moments with her partner! Curiously, and for reasons about which there can be only conjecture, "Moll" would never permit the patient to touch her breasts. Not that the patient really wished to with any intensity—it was just that they were "off limits," a situation that probably served to heighten the patient's vicarious pleasure as she identified with her partner.

It seems clear enough that despite all appearances to the contrary, the patient was the *penetrator* according to my classification for homosexuality. Parts of her body penetrated into the oral cavities of her partner. Whether she or her friend had been the prime mover, the one to supply the movement through which such anatomical relationships were established seems of no particular psychological importance. The outcome, rather than the means by which this was accomplished, is the more important. In similar fashion we see that the aggressive "Moll" was, considering the anatomical relationship, the one into whose body portions of the anatomy of the patient penetrated. She was, by my classification, the *receptor*.

There is a common bond of orality joining all "homosexuals" with each other. "Homosexual" behavior, irrespective of the manifest form it may assume, is classifiable on the basis of the anatomical relationship established between partners. But, as commonly occurs, the data finds support in other considerations as well. It is for this reason, and because the material is so very forthright, that I have chosen to present additional clinical considerations in this case which relate more specifically to the psychodynamics of the dream. It seems to me that to have presented it separately in a foregoing section would have resulted in fragmentation. Therefore, what immediately follows, though it explores further a "homosexuality," does so through the medium of the interpretation of a dream and the special significance accorded to the dream experience itself by this patient.

Prior to bringing in her first dream to therapy, the patient described the delight she took in "dreaming." She reported lying down for a "rest" with the purposeful intent of "dreaming." She looked forward to such occasions, experiencing them as the greatest of life's pleasures. There was no content—at least no verbal content—to these "dreams." In purposefully cultivating this experience she sought a blissful oblivion which she achieved by what she referred to as "self-hypnosis." This was the dream she brought.

"There was a huge figure— I could see the top part. It was like Mr. Clean. It was built like he is, but the bottom was hazy and I couldn't tell whether or not it was a man or a woman. 'Moll' stood behind this figure and peeked out at me and beckoned." (This "Mr. Clean" is a fictional character well-known because of extensive advertising and widespread use of a brand of detergent known as Mr. Clean.)

The patient's associations included a description of the disproportionate size and development of "Mr. Clean's" chest. She related "Mr. Clean" to her mother through her comment that the latter had a "big bosom." Thus, we learn that the manifest dream content of "Mr. Clean" stands in place of the patient's mother. The male characteristics of "Mr. Clean" are deemphasized, for the bottom part of the body is hazy as though to say, "It's what's at the top that is important." We understand that the exaggerated chest development of the dream figure is but a

143

way of presenting the idea of the mother's breast, appropriately disguised because of the forbiddingness of unconscious oral impulses directed towards it—the very same forbiddingness that forces the patient to take the role of *penetrator* in her overt relationship with "Moll" while all along she secretly indulges the fantasy of being the *receptor*. Her association was that her mother was forever "cleaning things up, scrubbing walls, insisting on neatness, and extremely concerned as far as personal cleanliness was concerned." And, from the position the patient assigned to "Moll" in her dream, we have no difficulty whatever in translating who "Moll" represents in the patient's unconscious. We had, of course, already suspected this from the patients account of her relationship and fantasies about this friend; now we find our supposition confirmed in the dream. The patient's agitated seeking and pacing and repetitive thought—"I won't survive without her"—doesn't fit very well into the circumstances of adulthood, but does exceedingly well in relationship to the patient's conflicts during the *weaning process*. As a matter of confirmed historical fact, the patient was breast fed by her mother until the age of eight and one-half months, so that the interpretation has a basis more substantial than is commonly the case.

We must, however, explain why the patient has "Moll" beckoning to her in this dream. In the dream "Moll," like "Mr. Clean" represents the patient's mother, so that the latter's importance is emphasized by doubling her symbolic representation. Recalling the patient's receptor fantasy when she played the *penetrator* role with "Moll," and recognizing that this behavior when interpreted said in effect, "It is not I who suckle, it is she," we are prepared to understand the significance of "Moll's" beckoning. In the dream the patient expresses her wish—long standing since infancy—that her mother continue to be the active one in their relationship. In terms of the *weaning process* the patient attempted to solve the paradox of attraction

144

as well as fear of *merging* by insisting that it was not *she* who wished to suckle, but her mother whose idea it was to have her suck! This is why "Moll" appeals to her. "Moll" fits precisely into the pattern of the patient's infantile solution to the *weaning process;* "Moll" is the aggressor. She provides the situation in which the patient can, under the guise of being the *penetrator,* actually obtain virtually all of her gratification from the fantasy of being what is to her a forbidden receptor attitude.

This patient did not terminate the *weaning process* by renouncing the wish to *merge* through fear of *merging.* Instead, she achieved the appearances of the *adult mode* by a circuitous route. She retained the oral urge to *merge,* but would have it that such was permissible into adult life under circumstances where oral incorporative wishes could be denied in reality while being indulged in fantasy. In this position (the very one she took with "Moll" in later years) she could disguise from herself that the wish to suckle was not a desire exclusively "Moll's." The direct confrontation of the ego with the urge to *merge* did not result, as is normally the case, in the rejection of the wish to *merge.* The infantile wish to *merge* at the oral level remained intact. Just as in the case of the male "homosexual," the original object of the oral impulse, the mother's breast, lurked under a disguise provided by the psyche. In this case the patient's own body became the object of her fantasied oral impulses. Of course, this becomes possible because the unconscious does not recognize ownership. Strictly speaking, it is the mother's breast which, having been the first object of oral incorporative impulses, remains forever after what is sought-for. Nor is it difficult to see the mechanics of this defensive maneuver. For during *merging* the ego boundaries simply dissolve. There is, while *merged,* no distinction made by the ego between the self and the breast. They become "one." This experience leads to the association linking mother to one's own self, an association taken advantage of in her relationship with "Moll" when she fantasies that she is once more an infant who, like "Moll," is "vigorously sucking.

It hardly needs to be said that there are severe marital discordancies in this case. Even their general directions could be predicted on the basis of what already has been discussed. The husband has strong "mothering" tendencies. He looks after his wife to the point of "forcing" the good things of life upon her. He, too, fits the pattern unconsciously desired by the patient. Like her own mother, he provides for her because it pleases him to do so. Her wishes do not concern him at all. He seeks out what he perceives to be her needs and does all he can to fulfill them. Her complaint is that he fulfills needs which in fact she does not have. Like her mother, he gives to please himself.

Insufficient material was available to throw light on the mother's behavior in relationship to completion of the patient's *weaning process*. I did learn that the latter was quite proud of her prowess as a cook, and that her feelings would be hurt if her family did not show their enthusiasm for her efforts by eating the portions served them. She also had a reputation for preparing food and delivering it whenever friends and neighbors became ill.

In my judgment "homosexuality" is a misnomer. The phenomenon would be far more accurately designated if it were called "homo-pseudosexuality," or to be phase-specific, "homorality." The early fixation would then be more readily recognized, and the manifestations understood to be oral incorporative *masquerading* in the disguise of sexuality.

In summary: Though at the time of his introduction to "homosexual relationships" the *penetrator homosexual* rejected an overt *receptor* role, nevertheless the urge to be the recipient of the body of another—as he was as an infant—remains deep within him. The clinical data I have described is, of course, limited, yet material of a quite similar nature and import is to be found wherever it is possible to examine "homosexual" individuals in depth. In my study of "homosexuals" there has not been an instance of either "penetrator homosexuality" or "receptor homosexuality" whose origins could not be traced to an arrest of the *weaning process*. I have found it helpful to approach the phenomenon of "homosexuality" from the point of view that the condition represents a compromise solution to a paradox arising during the evolution of that process. We see then that my formula for "homosexuality," depending as it does upon the functional relationship of the actual or fantasied nature of the physical relationship between participants, is universally applicable. It brings a satisfying degree of order and comprehension to a subject where emphasis has traditionally centered on the "sexual" manifestations.

The psychotherapy of such perverse practices is difficult at best. But casting the problem in terms of its ultimate psychological origins in the relationship of the *weaning process* has offered an advantageous frame of reference within which insight can be developed.

CHAPTER IX

The Origins of Schizophrenia

Schizophrenia, or schizophrenic reaction, is the diagnostic term for a syndrome with fairly well-defined characteristics. The reaction may be latent or symptomatic. It may impair psychic functioning but slightly, or involvement of the ego may be so extensive that complete withdrawal from the world of reality results. An exceedingly wide range of symptomatology is embraced by the term, but several subtypes are usually distinguished. These are the paranoid, catatonic, hebephrenic, simple, mixed, and undifferentiated. Each of these subtypes may be further described by appending to them the modifying adjectives acute, chronic; and still further by a judgment as to whether the condition is mild, moderate, or severe. The nomenclature is complicated by terms such as schizoid personality, pseudoneurotic schizophrenia, ambulatory schizophrenia, and even schizophrenic character—these representing efforts to bring order and comprehension to an area of human pathology where no therapy of curative value has yet been developed.

Hallucinations, delusions, impairment of affect and concrete thinking are considered characteristic. Ego deficits are sometimes subtle but constant accompaniments. The condition occurs at all levels of society, but because the problems of detection are difficult, distributional differences in race, age, and economic status are not accurately known. One gets the impression that low cultural levels are more heavily "loaded" with schizophrenics, but this may be the result of manifestations of the reactions being more readily detectable in one subculture than another.

The etiology is an enigma, for which reason incredibly

large and diverse numbers of "causes" have been proposed. The idea that the reaction is multidimensionally determined has been widely accepted. This may or may not be so, but such considerations do seem to lull one into believing that basic understanding has been achieved, when the major benefit of such a view has been a deepening of our respect for the complex ramifications of schizophrenia.

An extensive clinical review of schizophrenia is beyond the scope of this book. There are, however, several clinical observations having a bearing on the material which deserve recording. Even though a means to terminate the hallucinations so frequently present in schizophrenia is presented to the patient, he refuses, by one or another strategem, to employ it for such purposes. When at first he is advised how to terminate his hallucinations he cooperates fully, yet he does not continue this for long. He may complain of being "bothered by voices" or object to some other hallucinatory phenomenon, yet one cannot persuade him or motivate him to banish such experiences from his psyche for long, even when the means itself is painless and even intrinsically pleasurable. No other single clinical finding so firmly establishes the validity of the concept that hallucination and its sequela, delusion, serve a function useful and even essential in the schizophrenic's psyche.

Common to all schizophrenia is an impairment, subtle or obvious, of the ego's capacity to deal with instinctual impulses according to the *secondary process*. The immaturity of the ego is reflected in the manifold distortions observable in its relationship to objects, as well as in the ego's relationship with itself.

In my judgment the schizophrenic syndrome is the consequence of disturbances in the maturational process by virtue of which the ego develops. The idea that schizophrenia is a function of ego immaturity not only puts the condition in the light of being a kind of psychic deficiency syndrome, but also explains that the great variety of clinical manifestations is due to the fact that no ego function is exempt from inadequate performance. In an earlier chapter I identified and described the *weaning process,* demonstrating how the ego's growing alarm over the *merging* experience when suckling took place, caused it to seek what turned out to be a series of compromise solutions. *Merging* became transformed into *raptus* which in turn gave way to the *adult mode,* of eating and conducting one's self. The ego accomplishes a major feat when it finally divests the eating function of the libidinal qualities which earlier, when the infant ate according to the *infantile mode,* were so prominent.

The progressive differentiation characterizing the maturation of the ego extends over a long period of time, and for some individuals probably never ceases. A wide variety of influences, from internal as well as external origins, impinge upon it with varying degrees of effect. These influences vary in their effects, depending not only upon their nature but also on the attained status of the ego at the moment of impact. Consequently ego imperfections of all kinds could be anticipated were nothing more than these considerations taken into account. The very fact of exposure to life's buffetings would be expected to register effects upon the sensitive and responsive ego development process. One is not surprised then to find that the character of any particular event, and its time of impact in the developmental process, are critically significant.

The younger the ego the more impressionable it is to events it perceives as significant. This statement must be qualified by taking into account the fact that early in its development the ego is insufficiently organized to be influenced by circumstances which, if brought to bear later on, might be devastating to it. A particular stimulus, otherwise of indifferent influence on the just-established ego, may register as a trauma if its occurrence should coincide with some vulnerable moment in that process. The death of a father, for example, has no psychic meaning or representation in the mind of a week-old infant. But such a tragic occurrence at the height of efforts to find a solution to the enigma of the oedipal phase of development might, were the conditions right for it, seriously compromise psychosexual maturation. Or, consider that when a mature man misses a meal, no lasting or significant psychic significance will be registered. But when an infant is not fed when he is hungry, the experience may leave its mark in his psyche for a lifetime.

The particulars of a trauma, the stage of development at the time of impact, the previous experiences already passed through, the instant circumstances preceding, during, and after the trauma, all have interrelated and reciprocating feedback influences. For this reason it is not possible presently to catalogue "trauma" according to an order of significance nor in any way predict, save in broad overall ways, what if any effect any specific event might have on the *weaning process*. At this point in history the best we can do is to make observations after the fact. Schizophrenic symptoms, as well as a number of other aberrancies, evolve as a consequence of the stunting or impairment of ego development during a very specific period of infantile development. Trauma occurring after the *weaning process* has been completed, as evidenced by the repression of the *infantile mode* of eating, seems to affect the content rather than the structure of the ego. For just such reason the psychoneuroses are amenable—where the patient is motivated—to psychoanalytic therapy, whereas, the psychoses are not usually curable by any present technique of therapy. A person with hysterical paralysis of an arm can be cured, but one born without that arm must settle for a prosthesis. Where the *weaning process* is subject to persistent disturbances which prevent a shift to the *adult mode* of eating and conducting one's self in general, the very structure of the ego becomes irreparably stunted and its subsequent functioning compromised.

In Chapter VI I described the mechanics of the development of hallucinations and the manner in which these in turn evolved into delusions. I emphasized that the phenomena of hallucination and delusions are universal experiences, and that the critical feature by which the normal can be distinguished from the pathological is to be found in the modus operandi of the ego. Normally, hallucinatory phenomena are repressed, often so thoroughly that many deny on initial inquiry that they have ever experienced sensory perception for which there was no assignable physical cause. Yet in these same individuals a more precise inquiry, giving examples of what is intended by the word "hallucination," reveals an almost universal acknowledgement of such experiences. I also pointed out that the delusions of normal people are influenced—at least temporarily—by an appeal to the critical faculties of the ego. Even though a delusional idea might not be eschewed, the normal person can acknowledge the existence and validity of beliefs other than those held by himself. Steps by which ideas of reference and paranoid thinking develop from preceding hallucinatory experiences were likewise explained. The interrelationships between these phenomena were described and their origins traced back to events transpiring during the *weaning process*. The psychodynamics of the attainment of a mature ego having been formulated and provided with this background of understanding, we are prepared to consider the problem of the origin of schizophrenia, or—to put the matter in a way I prefer—the dynamics of ego immaturity. For I do not find clinical evidence that schizophrenia is the consequence of the collapse of an ego previously mature! The mature ego deals with whatever reality presents. The immature ego responds according to the degree and extent of the immaturity, to the impact of external reality, or the importunings of instinctual impulses. One of those ways we call "schizophrenia." It is by no means the only way in which ego immaturity reveals itself.

Our present-day nomenclature employs separate diagnostic categories for the varieties of character and behavior disorders, the immaturity reactions, and the personality disorders. These clinical conditions are but differing manifestations of a single disorder: early arrested development of the ego. Just as a physical injury has more extensive effects upon an organism the earlier in its development cellular trauma is introduced, so a psychologically traumatic event, or the selection of regressive solutions to *weaning paradoxes,* impairs a larger portion of the ego the earlier in the latter's development these take place. The symptoms of the foregoing diagnostic categories can be arranged in a spectrum, each segment of which can be correlated with relative specificity to phases through which the *weaning process* passes. It is understood, of course, that the earlier an ego deficiency is established, the more extensive the distortion in all subsequent ego functions. This rather oversimplifies the matter because no account is taken of the multiple and varied influences upon which depend in considerable measure the content eventually assumed by the ego.

In the case of schizophrenia, the symptomatology is dependent upon the phase of the *weaning process* at which the arrest of development takes place. Although this formulation offers insight into the origin of ego immaturity, it says nothing regarding the forces which shape the ultimate form of the ego's modus operandi. The "arresting event" in ego development it more complex than the expression implies. Indeed, these events cannot be identified outside of the psychological context within which they occur. Whether or not any particular element serves as an "arresting event" in the ego's maturation requires participation of other factors both within and outside the ego. Repetition of experiences arising outside the ego seem to have an important bearing on ego maturational impairment, but the degree and extent to which the ultimate shape of the ego can be ascribed to such reinforcement of an arresting factor cannot be estimated accurately. Despite the impossibility of defining circumstances external to the ego in terms of their being intrinsically "arresting events," it seems possible to recognize that some repetitive external circumstances have more potential to inhibit the maturation of the ego than others. This comes about because whatever effect an external event has, it is the ego's manner of dealing with stimuli impinging upon it which determines what the ultimate influence will be. We are fairly certain that repetition does not merely offer greater opportunity for the ego to respond regressively, for the ego is not a passive receptacle but responds according to the rules of unconscious *infantile logic*.

It can be shown that those who are to become schizophrenic have very particular outside influences brought to bear upon them very early in their lives. The independent wishes of their burgeoning egos seem to be disregarded by mothers who, for reasons peculiar to their own psyches, feed their infants according to a philosophy of which they are unaware. They suckle the infant according to their own estimate of the infant's requirements. They treat their children as though they didn't know enough either to recognize or communicate their own feelings of hunger. They deal with the child as though it were a plant to be watered rather than as another human being, albeit young, whose feelings are both unique and important. The attitude is, "Mother knows best and you know nothing." Such mothers nurse according to their own wishes rather than in response to the notification of need communicated by their infant. They act as though they know as much of their children's desires as they do about one of their own extremities! Indeed, one would not be far off the mark in saying that for such women their children are comprehended and related to as extensions of themselves, not as individuals with faces and souls of their own.

It is especially instructive to recognize how the attachments between mother and child are viewed from the point of view of an inarticulate infant. As time passes, the basic patterns of the schizophrenic mother's attitude does not change. Her behavior toward her child may seem to be different, thought most often her only modifications thereof are to bring her behavior into line with the circumstances imposed by the physical growth of her offspring. The woman driven to feed others, i.e., one who displays a distortion of the maternal impulses and as a consequence becomes obsessionally occupied with feeding, has had such feeding drives deeply imbedded in the matrix of her character. Each time of life has its own idiom of expression, but the theme of "there must be filling" remains constant, itself the consequence of early conditioning influences to which the mother herself perhaps was subjected.

A young schizophrenic patient of mine told me that he had asked his mother to bring him a bag of potato chips when next she came to visit him in his quarters at school. At the time he was living in a college dormitory, and though he could have supplied himself with potato chips without great inconvenience he chose, for unconscious reasons of his own, to ask her this favor. His mother appeared on the scene carrying not the bag of potato chips, but a shopping bag crammed with a variety of foods. What she did *not* bring were the potato chips! She brought him what she wanted him to have, not what he had asked for! This young man had come to see me in the first place because at the age of 16 the idea of growing up and leaving home filled him with consternation. His conscious wish was to be once again a little boy, a piece of ideation reinforced by a curious example of somatic compliance: his voice had assumed the timbre and some of the intonations of a small boy.

In another instance, a chronically ill schizophrenic girl —hospitalized for years—was visited regularly by her mother, who would make her weekly trek carrying a shopping bag filled to the top with packages of marshmallows! The patient herself cared little about them and, in any event, they were supplied in quantities far greater than she could have used even had she been partial to them.

Those who later become schizophrenic never have a normal emotional climate during infancy. For many years I looked into the matter with special interest each time I read in a patient's history that his or her early life had been "normal." Schizophrenia doesn't "just happen." In no instance, in my opinion, is the term "normal" applicable to the early life of a schizophrenic. Whether overt or covert, there are always discordancies with the family relationships, especially and specifically the mother-child interplay during the *weaning process.*

Most clinicians are quite aware of interpersonal distortions in the lives of schizophrenics. If these be "extrapolated" to the preverbal period of life, an important appreciation for the circumstances of the *weaning process* is possible. We are so used to taking at face value the judgments of relatives that it is no easy matter to come to the realization that if the patient's infantile relationships had been "normal" he would not have suffered that stunting of ego growth to which his symptoms are chargeable. On those occasions when I have had the opportunity to study the personalities of the mothers of schizophrenic individuals, I have been impressed by the extent of affective isolation and the severe limitations of the capacity to reciprocally relate to others. In a word, feedback—the mainstay of meaningful relationships—is not much of a factor in the personalities of such persons. There is an empty, hollow quality about them, a preoccupation with themselves which prevents their fully grasping the sense of things. Charm of the superficial, shallow type often produces an impression of attractiveness which, however, soon wears thin. They do not know the real meaning of appreciating another's feelings. Nor are their own feelings importantly influenced by perception of the reactions within others. This inadequacy of relatingness often becomes incredibly evident the older the mother grows. The kind of unfeelingness one sometimes detects in the aging mother of a schizophrenic seems to be a reliable indication of maternal attitudes from earlier times. The mother who brought the marshmallows would also send her hopelessly regressed daughter "get well" cards despite the fact that she had been repeatedly told by members of the medical staff exactly how things stood with her child. It wasn't that she disbelieved—it was rather that she did not listen to them despite her apparent interest in what they had to say. There is sometimes a quite subtle species of poor judgment, perhaps better recognized as credulity, which in effect is nothing less than inadequate reality-testing in one of its many guises.

Another mother of a schizophrenic told me, toward the end of a discussion we had about her son, "Oh, he's such a good, sweet, beautiful boy, doctor." The comment is perhaps unremarkable save for the fact that the patient was 23 years old and an uncommonly unattractive young man besides. This mother's behavior toward her son was predicated upon an inner image she retained from the past, or fabricated out of her own unconscious. She never saw him or "understood" him as a person in his own right, but rather conceived of him as an extension of herself.

What then are the special circumstances under the influence of which ego maturation is, so to speak, nipped in the bud during the *weaning process?* To observe the matter directly would require that we be privy to the workings of the infant's mind. This being patently impossible, we must learn by indirect and circumstantial evidence to reconstruct and put into articulate form the mechanism by which I consider the normal drive to maturity is coerced. From the data available I have drawn conclusions which represent not final judgments, but a logical theory by which to explain the genesis of immaturity.

We must assume that though ordinarily we do not

examine the mother of a schizophrenic until many years after the *weaning process* has been passed through by the patient, that the mother's basic position or philosophy has been long established and does not undergo any essential psychodynamic changes over the years. One acknowledges that the overt manifestations of character traits may be modified, but the basic configuration of the individual psyche does not change. Some of the clinical examples already cited suggest to us that even the manifestations of what is taken for motherliness remain unchanged through the years. It is not likely that spontaneous alterations in basic psychological pattern would very often be achieved, considering the well-recognized difficulties of modifying the "shape of the potter's design" no matter how skillful the psychotherapist. In fact, we are probably correct to discount such a possibility. So when we assume that the mother's present attitude and behavior are predicated on psychodynamic considerations identical with those holding at the time of the patient's infancy, we have considerable support for this supposition.

In the cases of the two mothers, already referred to, the self-gratifying urge to feed their offspring, even after the latter had achieved adulthood, could hardly have been more obvious. We may be reasonably certain that the same poor judgment and behavior unrelated to the realities which were present had been there at least for as long as they had been adults. These mothers are, in effect, "food-pushers." They force food on others not because others need or desire it, but only because of intense personal psychological needs of their own to behave in this manner.

Another schizophrenic's mother delights in her cooking skills. Whenever a guest, no matter who it may be, comes to see her she offers a sample of her cookery at the earliest opportunity. If her offer of refreshment is accepted she demonstrates her pleasure by hovering over her guests. If her hospitable offer is refused, however considerately, her feelings are hurt. She makes her displeasure quite evident, so that there can be no doubt in anyone's mind how she reacts to refusals. Because of this, it not infrequently happens that guests feel constrained to accept her offers even against their wishes.

The patient herself, when confronted with her mother's overwhelming demands that she "eat something," deals with them tangentially. In response to her mother's importunings that she eat something she will reply, "I'll have some later." Subsequently she contrives to "forget" her promise. Sometimes her mother observes this and becomes aggrieved at her daughter's "forgetfulness." Nothing suggests that the mother's position in relationship to food and feeding has changed over the years. It seems to go without saying—she must have "forced" milk upon her daughter when the latter was an infant, just as she now indiscriminately "pushes" food, oblivious to every desire but her own. She feeds others not because they need or even wish to be fed; she acts entirely out of inner psychological requirements uniquely her own, and proceeds to discharge these feelings without assessing the relevancy of her actions. In contrast, most mothers feed their infants because they indicate by their hunger cries that they need to be suckled. Customarily mothers are, in a word, servants of their infants' needs rather than slaves of their own psychological drives. Usually a mother feeds her infant because the latter evokes her desire to satisfy *its* wishes. The schizophrenogenic mother feeds her infant without particular regard for his need, but with attention primarily to the vicarious gratification of her own oral incorporative impulses. During the initial phase of the *weaning process* this particular orientation—that the child exists for the purpose of gratifying the "mothering" needs of the parent—has no discernible adverse effect on ego growth. If carried to extremes, distortion of the infantile concept of "cause-and-effect" is produced. The correct sequence of "cause-and-effect" cannot be solidly established in the psychic economy if this should be the case. As discussed earlier, when the mother nurses without regard to the infant's *hunger tide* (one of the manifestations of which is his hunger cry) then the psychological connection between nursing and relief of the feelings of hunger is not definitively established.

It must be remembered, of course, that what might be considered maternal overfeeding contains within it vast areas yet to be explored. Presumably, there is a relationship between the degree of time-irrelevant feeding and the extensiveness of subsequent ego immaturity. Moreover, the concept is complicated almost beyond belief because the infant's ego response is a variable measurable with difficulty if at all. As *merging* shifts to *raptus,* reflecting the struggle all infants go through in their attempts to solve the paradox created in their passage through the *weaning process,* the future schizophrenic is, in effect, not permitted to make his will prevail. He is fed by his mother *regardless* of his desires. In other words the resistance of the infant to the desire to *merge* is ruptured by forcing milk upon him *despite* a refusal to suckle.

When disregard for the infant's ego occurs repeatedly, the natural fear of *merging*—which evolved as a consequence of the experience of ego loss when suckling—is overcome. The infant comes through such conditioning to conceptualize that *merging* is not dangerous at all and can be indulged in at any time; that it serves as a pleasurable retreat from unpleasantness of all kinds. What normally is not rediscovered until the achievement of genital supremacy, and then in specific relationship with coitus, becomes a way of life for the developing future schizophrenic. Part of his ego remains immature in terms of the non-relinquishment of *merging.* A commitment to the gratifications of maturity having been evaded remain unachievable. The *adult mode* partially is achieved but as a superficial manner of being rather than as an integral manifestation of the character. Elements of the *infantile mode* remain in such intances, waiting in the wings as it were, ready to take the stage in response to internal or external events which, by virtue of their symbolic significance to the patient, evoke the "replay" of *weaning process* enigmas. The *infantile mode* comes to the fore, more or less disguised but always identifiable in regressive phenomena. It is no longer always found in specific relationship to food as it once was during the early phase of the *weaning process*. It is to be discovered in relationship to events which, through the associational connections formed on the basis of *infantile logic*, become equated with food. That is to say that the hallucinating, delusional schizophrenic represents a person "replaying" the *weaning process* scene of being *merged* in some degree. It is for this reason that "contact" is well-nigh impossible to establish with the regressed schizophrenic, He is *merged* and in this state knows or cares for nothing save what he experiences.

Clinically this is interpreted as "preoccupation," "vagueness," "flatness of affect," and "confusion." The hallucination then comes to fill what would otherwise be an intolerable experience of emptiness. The schizophrenic has never been curable because to cure him would require that his *weaning process* be carried to completion. Perhaps techniques can be developed which place the schizophrenic in an earlier psychic time so that the unfinished work of weaning can be accomplished. The schizophrenic is not motivated to eschew the gratifications of his *merged* state. He is perpetually attached to an inner representation of the mother's breast, and nothing we know will persuade him to completely renounce this "position." The residual longings to return to the halcyon time of infancy, so deeply hidden and disguised in normal people, is symbolically achieved in the modus operandi of schizophrenia. As one would expect from such impairments of the ego structure itself, the manifestations of this immaturity are woven into the very fabric of the personality. Thinking in accordance with *infantile logic* leads to concretism, poor judgment and especially credulousness, within which may be found delusional ideas of cause-and-effect. Autism is so obviously

161

a devotion to preoccupation with contentless affect that, more so than most symptoms, it is manifestly similar to merging.

One schizophrenic woman experienced what she called "thick eyes," on occasions related to hunger. She made a point of the fact that this was only her name for what was an indescribable sensation. On inquiry it was learned that "thick eyes" referred to a daydream-like state, with eyes open, yet unfocussed and essentially nonrecording.

Indeed, what we are actually seeing when we look at schizophrenia is a state of perpetual *merging*. *Raptus* is "replayed," it seems to me, in the catatonic form. The drooling or mouth retention of saliva is most reminiscent of infancy. A certain degree of accommodation to the demands of the mature part of the ego is maintained, except in the most regressed cases, so that the evidence for this formulation may not be immediately perceived. Indeed, the mature aspects of the ego may overshadow, the underlying immaturity to a considerable degree.

Take, for example, the "All-American" type adolescent who inexplicably develops psychotic symptomatology. The schizophrenia has been present all along, as retrospective reevaluations by acquaintances indicate, but the immaturity has not been considered important or characteristic. The schizophrenic is *merged* and finds in this state his principal source of libidinal gratification. There is a certain advantage, psychologically speaking, in finding the major sources of stimuli within oneself. The gratification of *merging* has the diffuse nature of oral pleasures rather than the specific delineated character of genital gratifications. And, most importantly, it is always and instantly available without the participation of outside objects. This is the reason why, in schizophrenics, there is a general disinclination to engage in sexual activity. When the *weaning process* has faltered, the result is a fixation and subsequent distortion of all psychological phenomena evolving subsequent to this circumstance.

It sometimes appears that an event in the outside world is connected with and evokes an acute schizophrenic reaction. Examination of the details, however, reveals that some unconscious complex connected with the *weaning process* has, in fact, been responsible for the overt display of immaturity which in certain patterns we call schizophrenia. We might characterize or define schizophrenia as an ego immaturity which, unlike other childish things, was not put aside as physical maturation took place.

I have written briefly of the influence of the mother on the *weaning process*. The question naturally arises, "Why is it, if what has been said is true, that only one or two in a sibship become overtly schizophrenic, and that only rarely do all the offspring of a so-called schizophrenogenic mother become overtly schizophrenic?" The question contains several unarticulated assumptions. The first is that schizophrenia exists only in clinically manifest form. It is not valid just to assume that the "normal" siblings of a schizophrenic have no immaturities in their characters. One would hardly expect that a social situation so severe as to deny ego maturation to one sibling would make for ego maturity in the others. Nonetheless, this does occur more frequently than not. The assumption that children can be brought up in precisely the same circumstances and have precisely identical experiences is one widely held by otherwise perceptive persons, reflecting a tendency to discredit the significance of the process by which the foundations of the psyche are shaped.

No two people can be brought up identically. The mother's behavior toward each child is modified and influenced by circumstances that are constantly in a state of flux. An infant's early experience is to some extent predicated upon his ordinal sibship position. A first child has a quite different early life than the fourteenth or even the second! The psychodynamics of the mother produce influences of no small magnitude in each child. She may concentrate her feeding impulses on one child, thus taking

163

pressure from subsequent ones to cling to the *infantile* *mode*. Or the youngest and last may be unconsciously infantilized for a variety of reasons. A train of events occurring during the *weaning process* has the effect of shaping the moldable human clay into the form it will hold throughout life. The time at which ego stunting occurs during psychosexual development is, in my judgment, within the limits of the *weaning process*. Development may, in various degrees and various directions, be such that though the forms of the ego be maintained, it is weak and delicate in its various parts, and lacking in stamina. This seems to be an important feature that sometimes leads to the erroneous conclusion that a certain person was "perfectly normal" and then "suddenly" became psychotic! This, of course, is never true, but circumstances give that impression because we are unaccustomed to note whether the fabric of others is close- or loosely-knit.

Earlier in our study we made the observation that hallucinations and their progeny, delusions, are universal experiences. But we also noted that there was a profound difference in the way in which a hallucination or a delusion was handled by the intact ego as contrasted with the way it is handled by an ego whose structure remains immature because of events encountered and dealt with in a particular way during the *weaning process*.

It will be recalled how the perception of one's own cry during the time when the *hunger tide* was in ebb from its high could be interpreted by the infant as the event which had caused hunger first to diminish and then to disappear. We saw too how the *merging* response with its libidinal gratification could be similarly related in the infant's psyche to the ebbing-away of hunger. The person with the intact ego—the ego which has repressed the wish to *merge* orally —likewise represses hallucinations arising either in the waking or sleeping state. But in an immature ego the wish to *merge* is imperfectly repressed, with the result that the individual, in a manner of speaking, is filled with the hallucination, the degree or content being specifically appropriate, as far as one can discover, to his or her own individual life experience. The hallucination-delusion becomes reinforced and gathers content from subsequent periods of psychosexual development. It becomes the nidus upon which may crystalize every sort of conflict. Indeed, for this very reason it frequently happens that the ego immaturity, without which schizophrenia cannot exist, is overshadowed by more coherent and comprehensible symptomatology. To put the matter in yet another way, schizophrenics are persons recruited from the ranks of those not fully weaned. The immobile catatonic schizophrenic, lost within himself, experiences vague, indescribable fantasies and hallucinations that make up his universe. His hallucinations and delusions serve to fill what would be an otherwise painful void. He has become the receptor of stimuli arising within his own body. This "something" proves, on analysis of its manifold manifestations and disguises, to be associatively related to the first object that filled and thus relieved him during his infancy—his mother's milk.

Immature egos sometimes maintain a superficial appearance of strength until assailed by some kind of "loss," "deprivation," "loneliness," or "emptiness." More frequently than not the "lost" circumstance has had a libidinal value of considerable importance to the individual. The hallucination and subsequent delusion arise to fill the newly established void. As a consequence the individual experiences a lessening of anxiety. The reader is aware that in acute overwhelming schizophrenia the anxiety can be very severe. Nonetheless, without the hallucination the anxiety would be even greater. One observes that as the delusion elaborates and involves more of the ego, the anxiety decreases. It is as though the schizophrenic were comforted by suckling on his own sensation, achieving a level of gratifying sensory input from which it is most difficult to dislodge him.

Schreber, in his "Memoirs of My Mental Illness," would be classified as schizophrenic by today's standards. It will be recalled that Freud came to the conclusion, from the evidence he found in Schreber's memoirs, that the latter had the wish to be a woman. Freud assumed this to mean woman in the sexual sense. But woman also has another role, as bearer and nurser of children. It was from Freud's conviction—that "woman" meant to Schreber what it means to all adults—that his theory was built, and this contention seems to have been supported by Schreber's narration of the fantasy that so shocked him: that he was a woman in sexual intercourse. It will also be recalled that Freud felt that the cause of Schreber's paranoia was the consequence of unacceptable homosexual impulses. We have seen how "homosexuality," whether in men or women, is a symbolic replay of the urge to *merge* once more with the mother's breast, and the oral incorporative urges are executed in various guises so as to defend against the awareness of the forbidden-because-dangerous oral *merging*. In Schreber's memoirs there was a passage in which Schreber described how he stood before a mirror and imagined himself to be a woman. To heighten the illusion he employed feminine adorment. He hallucinated having female breasts on his own chest. He did not mention the genitals, that part of the anatomy having no part to play in the hallucination-delusion of being a woman. Schreber was "filled" with visions of the female breast. This is the core, the raison d'etre for his psychosis. Of course, the idiom in which this central theme is repeatedly expressed was derived from his early childhood experiences. He had ostensibly been "weaned" as an infant. He gave the outward appearance of having achieved the *adult mode,* but this was a sham which, under the impact of disappointment and emptiness in his later life, was overwhelmed by his latent and powerful urge to *merge* with his mother's breast as once he had done. Indeed, Schreber was in an unremitting state of *mergement.* It was the breast he sought, and the primitive ego made little distinction between objects symbolizing the breast. Breasts, penis, male, female, God—all were equally the objects of his wish to incorporate.

Schreber's biggest and consistent complaint was about the intensity of the "tying-to-rays" which he believed bound him to God. The passage where Schreber accuses God of wanting to destroy his "manhood" cannot be taken literally, for we know now that the latent meaning is usually closer to the truth than the manifest meaning of a delusion. This idea—this way of giving tongue to non-verbal experiences—is identifiable as the distortion of the wish to be once again an infant, expressed as an accusation that his adulthood, i.e., "manhood," would be taken from him by another. In terms already discussed, he had it that he would be changed from a *penetrator* into a *receptor*. Oral wishes were expressed as genital fears. And then, of course, there is the aforementioned passage where Schreber fantasies how it would be to be in the position of a woman during coitus. The material is more informative if taken figuratively rather than literally. We know from our previous proposals concerning the latent significance of "homosexuality" that the basis of Schreber's fantasy was his wish to be once again a "receptor." In general, Schreber's illness was characterized by his creation of an enormous amount of sensory stimuli of which he was constantly the *receptor*. He lived in an unremitting state of *mergement*.

The theory I propose views the problem of schizophrenia from a somewhat limited orientation. It is presented as a manifestation of ego immaturity, said failure of maturation being directly traceable to distortions having their origins in the transactions of the *weaning process*. The symptoms are viewed as serving psychic functions which, content aside, are directed toward a persistent state of excitation. Now, the significance of a new theory should be measured by its contribution to enlightenment and understanding.

167

And even this is of small import unless it leads to the development of a therapeutic technique or, alternatively, points out the way in which development can be so influenced that cure or prevention becomes possible. I have referred to schizophrenia as a species of ego immaturity, in anticipation of introducing the idea that what we know as the "schizophrenias" are but variations on a theme having its origin in the vicissitudes of the *weaning process.*

The subcategories of schizophrenia—the paranoid, catatonic, hebephrenic, and simple types—are generally acknowledged to be unsatisfactory and only approximately applicable in specific clinical circumstances. A great range of overt manifestations are encompassed by the term "schizophrenia." It has long been recognized that the core of the difficulty seems to be constant no matter in what particular form the clinical features are displayed. The *merging response* to suckling becomes modified under the influence of the developing ego. From the third month the hypnotic-like gaze I have named *"raptus"* occupies a progressively larger portion of the infant's nursing time. The *merging,* so prominent in the early weeks of nursing, progressively decreases until at last it is observed only at the finish of the last bottle of the day. The *raptus* itself, progressively altered by the continued molding of the maturing ego, is in its turn displaced by the capacity to smile and respond to objects *even while nursing.* (One mother of my acquaintance said in reference to her daughter, "She used to upset me. I'd be giving her a bottle and smile at her and she'd smile right back at me and would stop nursing." (Her daughter was about nine months old when this phenomena began.) The final phase of the *weaning process* is accomplished when *merging* and *raptus* no longer accompany eating. When this happens the child matures to that degree where ego ascendency is sufficiently developed that he eats henceforth according to the *adult mode.*

A complex series of events occurs during the *weaning*

process. Unfortunately, the work of carrying through the process is not always successfully and completely accomplished. Difficulties are encountered during the *weaning process* which, when not surmounted by the ego, leave indelible imprints on the developing character structure. The *weaning process* converts the *infantile mode* into *the adult mode* accomplishing this at about the ninth month of life. During this considerable period of time opportunities for misadventure are many and, in any event, every *weaning* process is exquisitely unique in its details. Just as in biology, where the earlier an injury is sustained the more far-reaching the consequence on the growth of the organism, so in psychology the earlier a distortion of development occurs the more extensive the manifestation in later life. This seems to explain the great variations in the degrees of immaturity observed in adults. There is a reciprocal play between mother and infant during this period of development, not the least important element of which is the fact that from the infant's side there are no words, no language, none of the intellectual instruments which, to varying degrees, adults unconsciously utilize in mentation.

Paranoid symptoms arise from the infantile experience of hunger as reckoned according to specific formulations of infantile logic. I have already described the attitudes toward infants which, in my judgment, are characteristic of the mothers of those displaying symptoms of ego immaturity. They take the "position" of pleasing themselves and are relatively unresponsive to their infants as unique individuals having existences apart from themselves. From the infant's point of view, such a mother, because of what appears to him as her inconsistency, is inadequately and incompletely conceptualized as an object. When fed at her whim, or on a rigid schedule, rather than according to the rhythm of the child's hunger cycle, the infant has no way unequivocally to establish the association between hunger pangs and their relief by suckling. As has been established, the infant becomes aware of the sensation of hunger when the flow of the *hunger tide* exceeds the pain threshold. He begins to cry, but when the mother reacts not to her infant's communication of need but to her own conceptions of what he requires, the cause-and-effect relationship discussed earlier cannot be established. The natural course of the *hunger tide* ensures that after a time the sensation of hunger ceases, reflected in the fact that the child stops crying—an event that, incidentally, reinforces in the mother's mind the validity of her "position."

"See? Just as I knew! He wasn't hungry at all!" By the same *post hoc ergo propter hoc* reasoning, when the infant suckles after a period of maternal persuasion this is interpreted as validating the mother's view that she must have judged the state of his hunger more accurately than her child could have done for himself. We now understand that the infant was indeed hungry, but even as he cried the *hunger tide* began to ebb, falling in intensity below the pain threshold. The infant casts about, in a manner of speaking, for some association which will explain how his hunger became assuaged. The reader will recall that while hungry the infant perceives the sound of his own cry. Through the operations of *infantile logic* the infant associates the perception of his own voice with what, in his experience, has assuaged his hunger, i.e., milk. It appears to the infant that the "voice" he hears comes from one or both of two sources. What he hears from bone conduction seems to come from inside his own head. What he hears via air conduction and reflected from the walls of the room appears to be emanating from the reflecting surface. The psychological connections through which hallucinations serve the function of "filling" are thus established. How the commonplace phenomenon of hallucination will be dealt with by the psyche seems to depend entirely on the degree of maturity the ego attains. Where the boundaries of the ego are poorly demarcated and the distinction between fantasy and reality is hazy, the potential for elaboration of the hallucination and its progression to delusion is potentially present.

Clinical findings support the proposal that there are three routes by which the infant perceives the sound of his own cry. Auditory hallucinations arise from three sources, according to patients: (1) from inside their own heads; (2) from an external but specifically unidentifiable source; (3) from some specific environmental feature such as a radiator, radio, electric light bulb, etc. The first is a "replay" of the infantile cry transmitted via bone conduction. The second is the "replay" of infantile perception of his own cry via direct air conduction. The third is the "replay" of the infant's perception of his own cry as reflected back to him from his environment (and seeming to him for this reason to emanate from a specific source within that environment).

The hallucination is elaborated by the immature ego for the purpose of securing the continued input of stimuli. A patient of mine had an extensively organized delusional system regarding Negroes upon which he "fed." He observed, on his return from a very active and stimulating vacation, that "I guess I was so busy I didn't have time to think about it." The delusion was "put on the shelf" when more filling food for thought and stimulation was available. And through *infantile logic* the immature individual quickly comes to the conclusion that the "voice" coming (as he perceives it) from outside himself must naturally be spoken by some other person or being, the content being determined by events experienced after language has been established. The schizophrenic unconsciously "sets up" the situation wherein he is the receptor of stimuli arising from the outside. As the hallucination evolves more completely into the delusion he oftimes has it that he is being accused of being "homosexual." We have learned not to accept at face value the manifest meaning of a schizophrenic production, but to search beneath the surface for the unarticulated symbolic meaning. It is not just "homosexuality" in general that the patient believes others ascribe to him. In my experience the paranoid schizophrenic who harbors this particular delusion *always* believes himself to be accused of *receptor homosexuality.* I have neither read of nor come across a case in my own experience where the patient's delusion was that he was being accused of *penetrator homosexuality!* The patient feels himself accused of performing fellatio; never does he feel himself charged with seeking other men to perform fellatio on him. The patient uses this frame of reference to couch his delusion, thereby denying the real source and nature of wishes long since forbidden. His unconscious wish is to be once again a receptor of the breast. But between this and the ultimate delusion developed via *infantile logic,* a number of defensive barriers have been erected.

Years ago, while auditing the initial interview of a just-hospitalized male schizophrenic by a psychiatric resident, it developed that the precipitating event seemed to have been a date the patient had had the night before his hospitalization. He had made love to the girl, but since he had done this with other girls on previous occasions, it hardly seemed that sexual relations per se could have evoked so sudden a psychotic episode. The resident inquired in detail about the patient's lovemaking. He pursued the matter with great diligence. At one point he asked "And did you suck her breast?" No sooner had the question been asked than the patient slipped from his chair to the floor, his body twitching and trembling. He became completely inaccessible and contact could not be established until the following day. The reader familiar with clinical psychiatry will appreciate that this was a most dramatic and unexpected consequence. There is no question that "homosexual" conflicts are often involved in the psychodynamic of paranoid schizophrenia, but when closely investigated they seem to defend against frightening instinctual oral incorporative impulses.

To recapitulate: The schizophrenias are the manifestations of person-specific symbolic replays of unresolved paradoxes arising during the *weaning process*. There is a good reason for suggesting that all states of structural ego distortion be collectively considered "ego immaturity syndromes." For by so doing attention is drawn to the existence of a common origin for clinical states of the most diverse manifestations. Moreover, the conception that ego immaturity lies at the base of a wide display of symptomatology, directs our search for an effective prevention and modification with therapy more certainly.

Perhaps an analogy from another branch of medicine will help contribute meaning to the significance of this formulation. Syphilis is a disease having primary, secondary, tertiary, and quartenary lesions. Years pass between the appearance of the chancre and the secondary manifestations. An even longer lapse of time intervenes between the latter and the neurological involvements responsible for the tertiary symptoms. That a causal connection existed between the primary and the secondary and tertiary symptoms was not dreamed of in the early days of medicine. What we know now to be but different manifestations of a single disease were once considered unrelated to each other. Understandably, each of the "three diseases" was considered to be due to distinct and different causes. In time, there was speculation that the "three diseases" might, in actuality, be but differing manifestations of the same pathogen. The matter could not be settled until Schaudinn demonstrated the causal agent—the Treponema Pallida—in 1905. As a result, what had been disputed speculation became absolute certainty. Once the etiological agent had been identified, therapeutic efforts could be intelligently directed toward the cause. Without Schaudinn's discovery medicine might still be bumbling along, preoccupied with the peripheral clinical manifestations of syphilitic infection, instead of having already learned how to treat the disease by destroying the causative agent itself.

Given the fact of an ego's immaturity, what might be done to further its growth? Is it possible to complete a *weaning process* which has "hung fire" for many years? Can knowledge of the *weaning process* be employed prophylactically so that what is a natural drive in the direction of the *adult mode* of existence is encouraged? These and a dozen more questions immediately comes to the reader's mind. They cannot, of course, be answered in this pioneering endeavor. Perhaps therapy can become as rational in the "ego deficiency syndromes" as it is in the present-day therapy of syphilis. Knowledge of the *weaning process* suggests many experiments and studies.

The L.S.D. experience, so like what one might imagine *merging* to be when the infant suckles, may become utilizable as a predictable therapy. Or perhaps addiction to a euphoriant drug might be purposely created and the psychophysiological dependency upon it utilized as a means to complete the "stalled" *weaning process.*

CHAPTER X

Clinical Implications
of
The Weaning Process

Hallucination and its progeny delusion, by serving the function of filling what would otherwise be an intolerable psychological emptiness, suggests that the psyche, no less than the rest of nature, abhors a void. It is not easy to adjust to the idea that man is incessantly stimulus-hungry. As observers we are inextricably united with that which we are observing. So wedded are we to the necessity for constant sensory input, so essential is this for the effective functioning of our reality-testing, that we have an understandable tendency to ignore the fact. Like the air we breathe and upon which we depend for our lives, we do not even think of its presence, much less its necessity, until deprived of it. Most humans find nothing remarkable in the commonplace. There is a great tendency to accept "what is" without question or curiosity. The commonplace and universal events of life evoke far less interest than the bizarre, the rare, and the unusual. The philatelist seeks exceptional and unusual stamps, scorning the usual and finding them of value only because in their presence his collection is all the more remarkable. The coin collector likewise seeks something unusual, some rarity, some unusual mint mark or scarce coin.

I bring this to the reader's attention because it seems curious that the *weaning process* has not yet been the subject of a great deal of study. Perhaps more exhaustive search would have been rewarded, but I found no books devoted to the psychophysiology of weaning. Psychological responses occurring during the *weaning process* seem nuclear to so many subsequent reactions that it hardly seems credible that a matter of such significance could have been passed over on such a grand scale despite the fact it is nonverbal. The *weaning process* lasts in all about six months, during which time the transition from the *infantile mode* to the *adult mode* of response gradually takes place. I have discussed some of the choices forced upon the growing infant as a consequence of his changing response to the experience of *merging*. As might be expected during the course of any relatively long-term process, influences of many kinds modify and shape it. There appears to be a correlation between the phase of ego development at which regressive solutions to the enigmas created in the course of the *weaning process* are selected, and the nature of subsequent manifestations of ego immaturity. The precise interrelationship between what (for want of a better term) can be called the ego's "maturational status" and the external events to which that ego responds requires study in depth and detail. What appears to be an insurmountable difficulty is encountered when one attempts to assess the influence of internal psychological factors on the nascent ego of an infant who has no verbal means of communicating what he experiences either at the time or later.

I have introduced the idea that a great many—perhaps all—sensory complaints without physically demonstrable causes are simply somatic hallucinations, hastening to add that hallucinations occur regularly in everyday life and are not intrinsically indicative of psychosis or psychopathology. The idea has been advanced that all medicines have placebo effects irrespective of whatever pharmacological benefits they confer. A psychodynamic explanation for this exclusively human phenomenon linking it to the nursing experience has been proposed.

The patient is a 60-year-old social worker who had been living alone for three weeks in a small cottage. He had just lost a most gratifying job because the government program supporting it terminated. He had been to dinner with neighbors and, on returning to his house 50 yards away, had sat in his chair and looked at a canvas he had been painting. It was turned around and he saw a message written across it. He got up to read it but found it "all gibberish." He looked elsewhere in his house and found more messages written "all in gibberish." He recognized he was hallucinating, felt frightened, and called his sister. She took him to her home, where he had been living until he obtained the cottage.

The meal he ate preceding the hallucination had been most satisfying. During the course of the evening he had had two glasses of Rosé wine. He hated the thought of leaving good company and going back to the loneliness of his cottage. He left only because he felt it was the proper thing to do; he did not wish to overstay his welcome.

The patient's son is a nuclear physicist who "writes papers for journals." He has tried to read his son's work, but finds it "gibberish." He has had many fantasies of going to live with his son and his family, but has never suggested it because he fears interfering in their lives. While living alone he has cooked his own meals. He has lost five pounds because he has not been eating properly.

These are the immediately pertinent features and facts in this case. His hallucination occurred under, circumstances of affective hunger. The hallucination arose to to fill the emptiness created by his departure from warm and friendly neighbors. Thus the reason for the hallucination as a phenomenon is crystal clear. But there is content to the hallucination which interlocks with the fact of the phenomenon, for its analysis indicates the patient's solution to his "emptiness." The content needs to be considered as a "solution-in-being," a wish in the unconscious that he be confronted with writings "all in English but gibberish"—i.e., that he be with his son, whose papers he considers "gibberish."

Now, this man is not psychotic. His ego does not build the framework of a delusion upon the hallucination. He knows with certainty that the experience was a creation of his own mind, real to him at the time, but having no substantiality of its own. The clinical value of knowledge of such benign hallucinatory experience cannot be overestimated in terms of relieving people of the fear that because of such experiences they are going "mad." It is my hope that as a result of these developments physicians will consider the possibility that the patient suffers from what may be diagnosed as somatic hallucination when symptoms do not correspond to organic symptom patterns.

It is not difficult to appreciate that every complaint possessing no discoverable structural alteration has a specific psychological function—that of filling for the sufferer what would otherwise be an even more painful void. Nor can we lose sight of the complicating fact that organic symptomatology may also serve such a function. We have come to recognize that each and every experience of functional pain has a twofold symbolic meaning. It is at one and the same time a symbolic "replay" of the infantile hunger cry *and* a representation of the infantile wish to nurse at the breast, expressed as in the process of being fulfilled. It is this "neat packaging," so to speak, that creates such difficulty when the physician offers to abolish the somatic hallucination. The patient consciously seeks relief, yet at the same time "denies" relief to himself even when it is obtainable, giving the most remarkable excuses and rationalizations for not doing so.

A patient of mine complained that she becomes irritable and "nervous" when she gets the "shots" which relieve her of symptoms so vague she cannot define them. I reply that if she gets relief from so simple a means as a "shot" she should by all means avail herself of the benefits of the hormones the referring physican administers. "But I have to take them more often—every two weeks—to get any good out of them anymore. I used to have to get them only once

178

a month." I tell her that if they help her she should take them even more frequently if necessary. Moreover, I assure her that her physician would not administer anything which would harm her.

No, I don't want to," she replies. "I don't want to get into the habit of hormone shots all the time. And besides I read somewhere that hormones give you cancer." (i.e. the symptoms perform a function I need, all complaints to the contrary.)

Through study of the psychological ramifications of the *weaning process* we have probed briefly into the mechanism through which the faith healer, the chiropractor, the acupuncturist, and cultists of all varieties achieve their results in functional difficulties. Their successes and their failures are traceable, in my judgment, to associations established in the psyche during the *weaning process*. The discovery that eating or drinking modifies and often terminates hallucination can be directly applied to explain how the placebo, terminates the somatic hallucination. The filling function of the hallucination is performed more satisfactorily by a medicine which is not only real but has curative and satiating powers assigned in the patient's psyche. Hallucinations, somatic or otherwise, may be terminated by incorporative activity; that they cannot be thus disposed of for long seems to be the consequences of a psychological requirement for their retention.

It happens that a patient's conscious wishes to rid himself of an unpleasant sensation exist side-by-side with an even stronger unconscious need for "something-that-fills." In those persons whose ego structures are maldeveloped because they have never fully completed the *weaning process* there is a demand to be filled which is both imperative and constant. For this reason they feed on their own hallucinations, delusions, and contentless psychological preoccupations. Hallucinations may sometimes be abolished by some simple expedient such as "prescribing" candy, milk, or coffee which the hallucinator is to take each time he has the experience of which he complains. Initially the results of this "treatment" may be remarkable—the hallucinations either diminish or frequently disappear altogether. One might expect the patient to be appreciative of being relieved of his complaints. But shortly after the treatment's success a curious attitude invariably is observable: the patient "forgets," or is "too full," or "the voices weren't so bad." He no longer follows the doctor's "prescription," offering these or similar rationalizations for his neglect. Naturally the hallucinations return and the physician, though he knows what to do about them, is frustrated in his desire to "cure" the patient. For without the patient's cooperation and active participation in his own treatment, the results he hopes to achieve cannot be accomplished. It is not what patient and doctor desire, but the imperative needs of the patient's immature ego which decides the matter. In my experience the "decision" is always made in favor of the regressive position, presumably because the more primitive the mode of response, the larger the number of conflicting and contradictory aims simultaneously achieved. This economic consideration appears fundamental to the operations of the unconscious, providing as it does a maximum of satisfaction with a minimum of energy expended in attaining that satisfaction.

This estimate of the economic determinants seems to be true of all hallucinatory phenomena, no matter in which sensory modality they arise and irrespective of the degree of maturity of the individual in whom they originate. The reader has probably anticipated the potential usefulness of this clinical discovery in medical practice. For it means that a favorable (or unfavorable) response to placebo provides an indication of the extent hallucination plays in any specific presenting symptomatology. In this regard, however, there are further considerations which make the "placebo test" far more complex than, let us say, tests for glucose in urine.

A great many physicians have witnessed a particularly

dramatic demonstration of the effect of incorporative activity. For sometimes a hospital patient has complaints for which no organic cause has been discovered despite exhaustive clinical and laboratory investigations. Not only as a consequence of the disappointment inherent in diagnostic frustration, but in even larger measure because of the patient's carping demands, the individual is labeled as a "croc" (from crocodile tears—tears shed for effect rather than for "cause"). The "croc" has been given opiates for his pain and demands that the "shots" continue to be given but in larger doses and with greater frequency. The patient's immoderateness evokes anger in hospital personnel, and ultimately someone decides to put the genuineness of the complaints to the test. The doctor (on his own or at another's suggestion) prescribes a "shot" of sterile water. As everyone "in" on the experiment expects, the patient obtains the same relief from sterile water as from his previous medication. The conclusion is drawn that the diagnosis of "croc" is accurate and/or the patient is consciously and willfully malingering; his complaints are "fake." The negative feelings toward the patient are now viewed as having been justified. What explanation other than some shade of malingering can be offered?

The theory of hallucination alone can explain what has occurred in psychophysiological terms. The patient's symptoms, having no physical pathology to justify their presence, can on this basis alone be considered somatic hallucinations. Moreover, they are abolished by incorporative activity, a finding which further supports the view that the complaints are hallucinatory in nature. The personality of the patient is demanding and infantile. His immaturity displays itself not only in these characteristics, but also by the development of persistent somatic hallucinations which function to fill whatever internal feelings of emptiness he experiences. The placebo, being more palpable than hallucination, displaces the latter as a "something that fills." What the patient experiences as "relief" is no more than the substitution of a tangible "filler" for an intangible one. The pharmacological content of the "shot" is far less important than the symbolic meaning of the injection procedure itself. In symbolic terms, the "filling" is accomplished by an outside agent to whom the patient has assumed an unprotesting receptor attitude.

A woman patient on hormone replacement therapy, prescribed by her surgeon after complete surgical removal of uterus, tubes, and ovaries ten years earlier, was given "shots" of estrogen at monthly intervals. To make it more convenient for her, the physician prescribed the same medication to be taken by mouth. Whereas the "shots" had helped her symptoms of "hot flashes, irritability, and the sensation of being swollen," the same medication taken by mouth produced no beneficial effect whatever!

But doesn't this example contradict the proposition that incorporative activity terminates or ameliorates hallucination? Assuming the patient's symptoms to have hallucinatory elements, why should one species of incorporation be effective where another is not? (Assuming of course that the estrogen entered the bloodstream as well by one route as by another.) The answer I think is to be found in the difference, both real and symbolic, between the "shot" in the arm and the pill by mouth. In the case of the pill the patient had to participate actively in its incorporation. She had to open her mouth to receive it and then was required to perform the self-initiated swallowing. Knowing something of the vicissitudes of the oral aggressive impulses, perhaps we can be permitted to speculate that for some psychological reason in this woman's past, the "forbiddenness" of incorporation has become attached to oral aggression designed to obtain relief from discomfort. It seems reasonable to assume that this "forbiddenness" is related to conflicts revolving about the *weaning process*. Despite our inability to precisely identify the conflict which rages within her, we can recognize that the difference in response between getting a "shot" and taking the medication by mouth is based on psychological rather than physiological factors. When the patient receives a "shot" she can disavow, so to speak, the desire within her to incorporate. She is filled with the contents of the syringe without any active participation on her part other than presenting herself to the physician. *He* decides where, when, how, and how much of the "filler" shall be given. The patient's *infantile logic* fails to recognize that in both instances she herself is the receptor. The *infantile logic* grasps only the conclusion that to be given a "shot" is a submissive passive experience opposite to "aggressively" swallowing a pill. Thus, the pill does not perform the same function in this woman's psyche economy as does the "shot" which, from the infantile point of view, has been "forced upon her."

There are further details which I believe support this formulation. Her demand for "shots" has increased in tempo so that she feels she now "needs" them every two weeks. She obtains a "special" estrogen-in-oil preparation from another state despite the fact that it is a standard pharmacological item easily obtained locally. Moreover, if the "shot" is to have maximum beneficial effect the doctor has to give it in "just the right way." She complains, for instance, that the beneficial effect are nullified if he "pinches up the skin" in the process of administering the drug. The needle must be exactly 1½ inches long or the "shot" doesn't help! The reader immediately recognizes the irrelevance of these considerations in terms of reality, but he is also aware of pyschic pertinency for the patient in all these curious features, even if the meaning thereof cannot be reduced to idiomatic language. The response of hallucinatory phenomena to oral incorporative activity or its symbolic equivalent is so consistent that it may be employed diagnostically to determine if a complaint is principally organic in origin or entirely functional. For it is a curious fact, even though not much attention has been paid to it, that a great many patients who consult physicians do not follow the therapeutic measures advised. They either do not take the medication, or fail to follow instructions when they do. It is known that a considerable percentage of physicians' prescriptions are not even filled!

Any physician who prescribes medication can readily determine how often his orders are not followed. Take, for example, the situation wherein the patient is instructed to take pills three times a day after meals, and to return to the physician a week afterward. At his next visit he is asked how he is progressing and reports that he is fine: the medicine has really helped, but the symptoms, although lesser in degree, are nonetheless still bothersome. The doctor decides to question the patient further.

At first the patient says he has taken the medication as directed, but then he tells the physician that his complaint almost disappeared the very first day he took the pills as directed—"after meals." He felt so well, in fact, that he decided the following day to take the pills but twice, since it was obvious to him he did not require one after each meal! His complaint continued to cause discomfort but "he got by" without too much difficulty. The next day the patient decided one dose of medicine was enough and he took a pill "before breakfast." That afternoon the discomfort returned in full force so he took a pill then. After work he felt no better so he took another pill before dinner, and still another before retiring because he still experienced discomfort.

The doctor, on eliciting such a history, is understandably puzzled. The patient has come to him for relief of symptoms. He must have faith in him or he would not have come in the first place. The physician may well seek to understand what kept his patient from following the explicit instructions. If the patient had bought a cocktail mix he certainly would have followed the instructions on the bottles. Why doesn't he do so when it comes to the serious matter of his health? The patient says he did not take the pills precisely as directed because he feared "becoming addicted" or "getting into the habit of taking medi-

184

cine." So, because he can "stand" the discomfort he does not take the pills except when, in his judgment, he "has to."

The practicing physician may have neither time nor inclination to pursue what can only end in ill feelings between the patient and himself. So he simply accepts the explanation offered without further ado and may try again to treat the patient with the same drug, this time assuring him it is non-addictive and can be taken whenever the patient feels it is necessary to do so. We shall follow this curious train of events no further, but consider instead the transaction between this physician and his patient in terms of the psychodynamics involved.

If we stand off a bit and take an overview of what has occurred we observe that, if nothing else, the patient's manipulation of his medication has resulted in the continuance of his symptoms! The doctor's treatment was designed to provide relief, and when it proved to be efficacious the patient promptly took the pills according to a schedule *of his own design,* so tailored by his unconscious that symptoms would occur despite the medication! In other words, like the hallucinated psychotic he dealt with the offer to terminate his complaint—his somatic hallucination—in a precisely similar manner. He neglected to follow simple instructions, when in doing so the medication demonstrably terminated the sensory phenomenon for the relief of which he had avowedly sought out the physician. He followed instead a compromising course unconsciously aimed at attaining both pill *and* pain.

Nor do a doctor's remonstrances that his orders have not been followed generally make impressions great enough to persuade such patients to alter their curious behavior. They are bound and determined to follow their own bent, and no reason or logic is ordinarily successful in persuading them to do otherwise. They simply refuse to examine the matter, believing their rationalizations sufficient unto themselves. Though their "reasons" will not stand up under close scrutiny, such patients seem incapable of recognizing the contradictory nature of their behavior.

Let us consider another example. A patient complains, let us say, of a headache or a backache, or perhaps an abdominal discomfort, the location of which he indicates in general terms and whose character he describes in vague, uncertain phrases. He say he experiences the discomfort "all of the time." Nothing relieves it or makes it worse.

Because of the information that nothing has an influence on the perception of discomfort we are prepared to discount our first impression: that we might be dealing with a somatic hallucination. Still, the pain does not fit the pain patterns of organic symptoms with which we are familiar. To clarify the situation we question the sufferer in greater detail, maintaining a particular awareness of what poor witnesses human beings are even unto their own sufferings. We do not unqualifiedly accept the proffered generalizations that the patient provides as to duration, quality, and even location of his symptoms. When the patient says his discomfort is present "all the time" we double-check the assertion. It may, of course, be precisely as he claims, but clinical experience suggests that most symptoms vary in intensity from one occasion to the next. The simplest clarifying technique is to study the patient from the time he awakes, tracing his daily activity through each of its steps and assessing his symptoms accordingly.

Was the symptom present at the instant he awoke? Or did it begin when he arose, or when he began to shave, or when he sat down at table, or as he ate breakfast, or after he had eaten? What happened to the pain when he drove his car out of the garage? What did he feel as he neared his office? When he actually entered it? When he greeted his boss? The idea, I think, is clear enough, and this investigative procedure very frequently reveals that the patient has not paid the least attention to the relationship of his symptoms to other events in his life. Of course, he has no self-evident reason for doing so. Nonetheless, he cannot truthfully answer even such a simple question as to whether the symptom was present the moment he awoke, or whether he ate lunch and it disappeared for a time. He doesn't often remember such details because he has been unaware of them. The examiner must be aware that the patient often will give a reply just to please. Such responses may have the ring of veracity, especially if the person making inquiry is not inclined to pursue clinical material in detail and assumes the patient's replies are based on careful self-observation. Indeed, in studying such phenomena, even if one instructs the patient to keep a record of his experiences the suggestion is often resisted rather firmly. Patients want relief, they say, *not* understanding! And such detailed history-taking irritates and annoys them. They demand "results" which they feel the physician can confer without further ado. But sometimes a patient comes along who is as curious as the physician as to why he experiences what he does and who grasps the idea that rational therapy is precluded unless the origin of a symptom is understood.

Let us assume that our model patient is thoroughly examined both physically and by clinical tests and that the results are inconclusive. Let us assume further that our detailed examination reveals the interesting observation that when he drinks a bottle of beer the discomfort (the location of which makes no difference in this example) vanishes! From these considerations the physician makes a provisional diagnosis of "somatic hallucination." He now proceeds with a "therapeutic test." He prescribes a pharmacologically inert pill and has the patient return after a three-day trial. Our model patient is worse—his symptoms have increased! The pills not only seem to provide no relief, but to bring on the discomfort as well! The doctor knows that the first, second, or even the third placebo attempt may be ineffective or even lead to an increase of symptoms, but that placebo has the capability of abolishing hallucinatory phenomena when circumstances are favorable. So the doctor, explaining to the patient that occurrences such as he experienced are rare, administers another placebo, different in appearance from the first. And, on this try, both the patient and physician are gratified with the "excellent results" attending treatment. Now the diagnosis of "somatic hallucination" has been confirmed, I should say, and though this is what we were illustrating, the experiment has yet more to teach us.

Our model patient has not only been correctly diagnosed but "cured" as well. How can a placebo, its potency no more than a figment in the patient's mind, produce a "cure?" The "miracle" of cure, though no pharmacologically active substance was administered, is no miracle at all! One must reckon with the fact that all along there has been much going on in the patient's life. His "medicine" was but a small albeit important part. The somatic hallucination arose in the first place to fill some kind of real or affective emptiness which the patient had experienced in his life. The placebo served in a more economical fashion the function of the hallucination which it displaced. Meanwhile, in his real life the patient's ego has achieved a more satisfactory equilibrium, one in which the previous void—responsible for the symptoms in the first place—has been effaced by some shift of real life activity, attitude, or fantasy. As a matter of fact, a great many such readjustments take place, and symptoms consequently disappear without medical assistance being sought.

It is commonplace, of course, for a patient to be hospitalized for laboratory study of a complaint for which no cause is ever discovered. But after the tests have been performed he returns home "improved" or "cured" without any specific therapy. Such patients are disinterested, and the physician is too busy to wonder very much why the patient "recovered." Analogous factors operate in these instances, as in the preceding example. Lay people harbor a different concept of "hospital" than physicians. For many just being in hospital puts the stamp of organic disease on what may in fact be somatic hallucinations. To "get well" after hospitalization is only to be expected. So we can see that hospitalization itself has a placebo effect of considerable importance. And of course, when one is hospitalized the environment to which he returns is different, perhaps substantially so, from that which he left. A change in post-hospital life frequently serves to fill the "void" which generated a somatic hallucination in the first place. And what observer of a hospital milieu can fail to see the sympathy and kindness shown to the sick? In this setting there is constant reaffirmation of being cared-for, an experience often providing profound therapeutic reverberations.

Few doctors are willing to prescribe an out-and-out placebo. For who wishes to become the target of a patient's anger were it ever revealed that he had been "tricked" into getting well? Besides, one avoids a charge of charlatanism if he administers medication which has at least a nominal pharmaceutical effect.

Another example will serve to illustrate a different direction of a patient's response to placebo. This man complains of headaches which began shortly after the birth of his first child. He did not give that event as the starting point; its relationship to the onset of symptoms was learned only by careful exploration. He has no awareness that the birth of his son has evoked feelings within him which he first experienced at the age of three. That was his age when his brother was born. He had, until then, been his parents' only child. Not only was his position in the home challenged by his brother's arrival, but his mother's attention, until then exclusively his, had to be shared henceforth. It is not difficult to imagine how he felt; undoubtedly he experienced intense feelings of rivalry. These, however, have been pretty well repressed over the years.

He had been married but a year when his son was born.

His wife had stopped working in the eighth month of her pregnancy, fully resolved to devote herself to keeping house for her family. The husband had greatly enjoyed the extra income her efforts outside the home produced, but he also liked the fact that she now stayed home. Nor was the fact that she had given up her job the only change in his household. His wife was so busy caring for the infant that there was even less of her time devoted to him —or so he felt—than when she had been employed. He admired her for being an attentive mother, but without being aware of it he also resented the fact that her being so was achieved in some measure at his expense. Whereas before he had been the center of his wife's emotional world, he now reckoned himself to be playing "second fiddle."

The couple had got along well since their marriage. Nothing turned up in the investigation of their relationship which indicated any friction between them. In fact, the only overt evidence that all was not well was the onset of his illness. The headaches seemed to occur in the evening, after he had returned home for the day. While he was at work he was free of them. At his wife's behest he consulted a physician. When the overall pattern of his living circumstances was investigated it was learned that his wife breast fed their child. There being no one else about, she nursed the infant quite openly in his presence. As far as he was aware, this occasioned no feelings—adverse or otherwise—on his part. The doctor told him his headaches were due to "overconcern." He prescribed some capsules, telling him that his medication would relieve his tension, and the headache which was a consequence thereof. He was instructed to take one capsule whenever he experienced headache. This could be repeated in two hours if necessary.

The "drug" was a placebo. The doctor thought there was probably some relationship between unconscious feelings in regard to being the father of a child and the symptom of headache. The description the patient gave of his "headache" was sufficiently bizarre in its own right to suggest that the symptom was, in fact, a somatic hallucination. It had none of the qualities associated with organic disease. The physician had considered allergy, though he felt such a cause unlikely. He kept that diagnosis as a possibility to be investigated more fully if his "placebo test" should prove unrevealing. The patient was instructed to return to his doctor in one week.

The following evening, however, he called the physician at his home. He had followed the doctor's instructions. After he had gotten home from work and had started eating his supper, the "headache" started. He took one capsule as he had been instructed, but immediately thereafter he became nauseated. That was the reason he gave for having called the doctor. He was angry because he had taken the medication only to make him feel worse. He had had headache but he had never been nauseated before! It must have been the capsules that did this to him, he complained, and if the doctor had any more medication like this capsule—well, he could keep it—he'd rather have the headache. The doctor asked him about the headache. Well, to tell the truth it's gone. But my God doctor, if I have to feel this way . . . don't you have something else to give me? Maybe I'm allergic to them or something."

We note with a good deal of interest that the *symptom had disappeared.* That there is another symptom—the nausea—seemingly in the forefront is another matter. The headache has vanished, though the patient has been inattentive to this fact. The dramatic nature of the "side effect" of nausea has served to focus attention on the latter; the remarkable fact that the "headache" has yielded to the placebo has evaded observation. The physician, knowing that there were no active pharmacological properties in the capsules he prescribed, had no cause to speculate whether the patient's surprising response might be due to a drug reaction. He knew with certainty that

191

what had taken place could be attributed to conflicts within the patient's psyche. The doctor asked how soon after the capsule had been taken that the nausea occurred.

"Right away, doctor—I'd no sooner gotten it down than I felt I was going to be sick right there at the table. I even got up and went to the bathroom." The medical reader is familiar with the fact that time is required for a capsule to dissolve and its contents absorbed into the bloodstream. An instant reaction—even if we did not already know that no drug was swallowed—must of necessity reflect a psychological rather than a physiological response. Our physician has now established the diagnosis of hallucinated headache. And from his experience he recognizes that if he urges his patient to continue the medication as originally directed, he will refuse to do so despite every assurance that the "side effects" he complains of are temporary. So instead the physician instructs the patient to discontinue the medication—which had "cured" the headache but at the cost of a worse discomfort—and to go to the pharmacy and obtain another medication which he, in the meantime, will order by phone. Having obtained the "new" medication (again a placebo but one different in color and shape from the original "medication") the patient feels mollified: the doctor, by his concern, has proved his interest in him. The patient has finally extracted from the doctor what he needs. When he takes the second precription it "works." His headache disappears and the "cure" is not accompanied by side effects.

The patient subsequently refers jokingly to the first medication when he again visits the physician. But despite the jocularity, the unhappiness and turmoil the doctor has allegedly put him through appears in the slightly chiding manner he takes toward the doctor. His attitude implies that if the doctor had been really interested to begin with, the "therapeutic disaster" brought about by the first medicine would have been avoided. And along with this is another attitude, the feeling of having won over the physician, of having extracted something which had at first been withheld. After all, *infantile logic* declares he could have given the right medicine in the first place. Oh, well! The point is that he *did* manage after all to get what he needed. Those new capules took care of the matter! Old doc may have gone off the track the first time, but when you come right down to it he came through with the right stuff!

Meanwhile, of course, a good deal has been going on in the patient's environment. His wife had become concerned when her husband had the attack of nausea; in fact, *she had stopped nursing the baby to follow him into the bathroom* to see if she could be of help. She had a few unkind words to offer about the doctor. She tells her husband that the latter should have known better than to "experiment" upon him with those pills. He should have prescribed the capsules to begin with! The placebo effect has now been reinforced by another kind of "filling." The fact that his wife took their infant from the breast to tend to him "proved" her willingness to give him "first billing" if his appeal were couched in sufficiently persuasive terms.

Psychodynamically speaking, the patient developed the head complaints because the birth of his child evoked long-repressed feelings he had actually experienced when he was a small child. Seeing the infant breast fed evoked wishes dormant since his own infancy. As a child he had seen his brother appear to be more favored than himself, and he longed to rid himself of the sibling who had, he felt, displaced him in his mother's affection. If he had overtly revealed the hostility he felt toward his baby brother, that would have angered his mother and thus made matters worse! The conflict was never solved. It was, however, successfully put aside so that no one, including himself, could even guess the intensity and direction of his feeling. The "headache" was triggered in its present context by its similarity with the earlier situation. He experienced a relative "emptiness" when he compared his own supper with the baby's. The sight of a nursing infant evoked long dormant feelings connected with his unresolved rivalry with his brother during early infancy. Though the reader recognizes the patient suffered a relatively small if any decrease in his wife's attentiveness, in the patient's unconscious where "the part equals the whole" any loss is experienced as total loss. The somatic hallucination then evolved to fill what would otherwise continue as a painful sense of emptiness. The hallucinated headache served concurrently as a vehicle to express the idea, derived from the operation of *infantile logic,* that his feelings of rivalry were responsible for and produced the situation wherein his brother was given that which had formerly belonged exclusively to himself. What required renunciation was the infantile rage and the associated destructive impulses originally directed toward his infant brother.

The transaction with the physician becomes the more meaningful once the patient's operational framework is understood. The appeal to the doctor with the request that his discomfort be ameliorated is a symbolic replay of the infantile cry which served an analogous function when, because of hunger, he cried as an infant. The puzzling "effects" of the medication in "causing" nausea require explanation. One would think he would be grateful in the present instance for a symbolic analogue of the milk which eased the infantile hunger pangs in his childhood. Yet he becomes nauseated the instant he swallows it.

The reader will recall that during the *weaning process* ambivalent feelings evolve regarding suckling. On the one hand nursing relieves feelings of hunger, which is reinforced by the "bonus" of the libidinal gratification of *merging.* On the other hand the ego, being threatened by the loss of its integrity because of that *merging,* rejects the idea of succumbing to the temptation to suckle according to the *infantile mode.* With this reminder of the dynamics of the *weaning process* we can see how first one side and then the other side of the ambivalence is expressed.

The first placebo was rejected—a replay of the *weaning process* conflict. His nausea when articulated says, "Who? Me want to incorporate something? Nothing could be further from my wish and I emphasize this by rejecting the very suggestion out of hand. See? I want to vomit it the moment I swallow it." The second placebo differs from the first not only in physical appearance but, importantly, in the details of its administration. We already know the consequences of his first demand for something which, when incorporated, would relieve his discomfort. The doctor prescribes the second medication in such a manner that it can be interpreted by the patient both as being administered *over the doctor's objections* and as something previously withheld. In the primitive sense, so well grasped by the unconscious, the ego could consequently take the psychological position that, "It is not I who demands that I be given something to take, it is the doctor who insists that I swallow these capsules. After all, what can one do in the face of his authority but follow orders?" The patient is "replaying" in modern-day terms and symbols a circumstance he "knew" as an infant. His mother probably "forced" him to nurse despite his protest. Within the totality of the present-day transaction with the physician he presents data enabling the doctor to understand the details of the preverbal *weaning process*. Those symptoms identifiable as somatic hallucination in the patient's unconscious represent an ongoing nursing episode: the patient being "filled" with sensory stimuli now, as when an infant he incorporated milk which "filled" his stomach. The doctor, symbolic of the mother of his infancy in the patient's unconscious, is sought out by him in the belief that the physician can interrupt or terminate the discomfort of the symptom by some means, traditionally the administration or provision of medicine. The circumstances of the *weaning process*, wherein milk is sought to relieve the hunger pangs,

195

is in this manner symbolically represented as the "replay" continues. The doctor wants to stop the hallucination (as does the mature part of the patient's ego) but these efforts are balked by the immature ego which demands more—not less—"filling" with sensory stimuli. The patient's behavior says, in effect, "It isn't true I have to relinquish the infantile mode of eating. All that needs to be done is to make it *appear* that it has been put aside." The patient all along covertly wished to indulge in the *infantile mode* of eating. This symptom is a compromise wherein, as economically as possible, the immature segments of the ego attempt to approach *merging* without suffering the anxiety attendant upon it.

The partial incompleteness of the *weaning process* seems clear enough in this example, the manifestations being related to the extent of ego immaturity. In the model transactions earlier presented the doctor gave a "pure" placebo in treating the patient's complaint. No part of the reactions subsequent thereto could be laid to the placebo per se. Confusion naturally arises as to which effects of medication are attributable to the "active" ingredient and which to the placebo effect. The study of a completely irrational therapeutic procedure has the advantage of providing an example of placebo effect in "pure culture." What is accomplished in the modification of symptoms in such practices can be exclusively attributed to the placebo.

Acupuncture, as an example, is a theory and technique of medical practice which operates on the assumption that the organs of the body and functions thereof are mediated and controlled by specific body loci. Under this system of medicine, disease are treated by placing needles of different materials into the body at specific locations at different depths for varying periods of time. This procedure favorably influences the symptoms with such regularity that it has been highly regarded in the Orient for centuries. Nor can there be any doubt of the method's efficacy, at least in the Eastern cultural settings where it is practiced today. The procedure has, for all its claims, no rational basis, yet an apparent influence even on organic pathological conditions has been claimed.

What must be explained, of course, is the singular circumstance that a medical practice based upon an obvious delusion can have any effectiveness at all in the treatment of illness. There are, of course, the natural recuperative powers of the body which tend to counter any disease process. Then, too, the factor of coincidence undoubtedly plays a significant part in those "cures" produced by acupuncture. But this hardly constitutes the entire explanation! Nor is there any miracle at work. The whole effect is to be attributed to the placebo component of the procedure. It is undeniable that afferent sensory impulses reach the central nervous system when each needle is inserted, and for the period of its insertion there can be no doubt that the patient has an awareness of being "filled" with something that, as far he is concerned, emanates from the needle. It seems highly probably that the patient has assumed, under these circumstances, the receptor attitude of taking into his body once again something which originates from the outside.

The "emptiness" which evoked the functional part of the patient's symptoms is replaced by the physical measures undertaken, and these are supplemented by his expectations for continuing benefits—expectations which are artfully and impressively encouraged by the circumstances under which "therapy" is administered. In our own culture, chiropractic holds a similar position and offers substantially the same benefits to the credulous. According to this curious theory, all diseases arise because of "pressures" bearing on the spinal nerves. The manipulations of the chiropractor, it is claimed, relieves these pressures, thus permitting the disease process to be reversed. The basis for chiropractic lies not in its claims, but in the simple fact that its methods provide a placebo effect. The fact is that chiropractic survives in our modern world only

197

because patients, from their points of view, have been treated successfully through its manipulations.

The fact of symptomatic relief from a procedure which has no demonstrable rationale is striking evidence of the power of placebo. The sucking instinct—the desire to be the receptor of stimuli—is tangentially and acceptably satiated as a consequence of the manipulations of chiropractic. Under the guise of "therapy" physically adult people can indulge unsated infantile strivings under the hands of the chiropractor who, in the patient's unconscious, has assumed the position once held by the mother. Curiously, chiropractic is often described by patients as methodology contrasting to that employed by a medical doctor. The latter, it is implied, just didn't know how to do things right! In the first place he "didn't know what was wrong," while the chiropractor "knew right away" that a "nerve was being pressed upon." He even demonstrated where the trouble was by showing the patient first an X-ray, and then a model or even a real spine where pieces of rubber tubes representing "nerves" can be shown being "pinched." Moreover, the chiropractor "did something." The patient can tell this from the cracking noise made when the "pressure was taken off the nerve" by the chiropractor's "adjustment." It sounds and is incredibly naïve.

Knowledge of the psychology of the *weaning process* is of importance in establishing valid psychodynamic formulations in a number of clinical situations. The acute "free-floating" anxiety attack without content seems to be a "replay" of anxieties experienced during the weaning process, reawakened in response to some evoking event in the patient's life. It is "contentless" precisely because the originating conflict occurred so early in life that verbal symbols did not yet exist. The patient's sensations are simply not translatable into language, though he strives mightily to bring them under the domination of his intellect. For economic reasons conflicts from later periods of psychosexual development come to attach themselves to the nucleus of anxiety already formed. The acute so-called "homosexual panic" invariably has for its content the fantasy of being a *receptor homosexual*. This appears to be a psychological formulation less frightening and hence more acceptable to the ego for the designation of unconscious infantile sucking impulse with its accompanying urge to *merge* than the more direct expressions of the desire to suckle according to the *infantile mode*. To repeat, I have never seen a patient who feared he was a *"penetrator homosexual."* The manifest fear is always of being a *receptor*. And the fear disguises *not* the wish to be "homosexual" but the more elemental wish to suckle and *merge,* together with the fear of ego dissolution attendant upon the imperfectly repressed infantile wish.

The analysis of the *weaning process* involves grappling with technical problems of considerable magnitude. In the first place the therapist must not expect the patient to recover any conscious verbal memory of the events of his own *weaning process.* Such memories as are verbalized are always retrospective formulations, erroneously ascribed to the preverbal period of life. For memory can be stored in verbal symbols only after language has been acquired. Hence the experiences of living prior to the development of speech are beyond verbal articulation. Thus "speculation"—the "wild analysis" that is so rightfully condemned as poor practice in the psychoanalysis of conflicts of post-weaning period origin—is an absolute requirement for the analysis of pre-verbal conflicts! In the solution of problems having their origins in unresolved *weaning process* conflicts, one must employ a rather different technique than that so widely accepted as desirable in the therapy of developmental difficulties arising after the acquisition of speech. Successful psychoanalysis of the *weaning process* period demands a degree of participation on the part of the doctor not favorably countenanced in psychoanalytic training. The unfortunate patient will never hit upon memories that were repressed even before they could have

199

verbal representation in the psyche through free association. He must be told how it must have been when he was an infant, and at the same time the transference which manifests itself as nonverbal attitudes toward the doctor must be kept under careful scrutiny and interpreted in terms of the preverbal conflicts which are conveyed therein. The analysis of the *weaning process* is in fact not "wild analysis" but rather "deductive analysis." And I suppose the most important part of the therapeutic transaction is the willingness of the doctor to be wrong on those occasions when, despite his most intelligent and perceptive efforts at reconstruction, his interpretations fall short of the mark.

Just the recognition of the existence of *weaning process* fixations extends our diagnostic capabilities and better determines the advisability of offering psychotherapy in questionable situations.

Take, for example, the following case. A 25-year-old man had had nocturnal epilepsy since the age of sixteen. His seizures started quite suddenly one night, and for the following two months or so he was "quite sick" with weakness, lassitude and what appears in retrospect to have been depression. He recovered from the depression after an undetermined length of time, and it has always been assumed that the depressive symptoms were preceded by the "seizures," though when the facts were carefully studied the reverse proved to be true. He enlisted in the Air Force, fraudulently disclaiming ever having had seizures. He served for two months before his nocturnal convulsive episodes came to medical attention and he was discharged. He has been advised to seek psychiatric consultation because of a recent increase in the frequency of his seizures. The dosage of Dilantin and Phenobarbital had been increased, but there was no corresponding decrease in the frequency or severity of his seizures. The patient learns of having had seizures only if, by chance, he bites his tongue or lip or if, as occurred while he was in the Air Force, the convulsion has been witnessed by others.

When he was a child of five he succumbed to the importunings of an old man and performed fellatio, repeating the act on several occasions but finally giving up the practice because he "thought it was wrong."

The seizures originated immediately after he had been rejected by a girl whom he "loved." Having recently moved into his community, she was a transferee to his high school class. The first time he saw her he experienced a powerful attraction unlike anything he had known. It struck him as odd that he should feel so strongly when "I didn't even know her name." He took her to one school dance and to two movies. There was little talk between them and the attraction was clearly one-sided. The only physical contact between them was incidental to dancing. His voice breaks in tearful self-pity as he relates the story of his disappointment. She told him, in effect, that she didn't wish to be tied to one boy and that she considered an exclusive relationship with him was out of the question. He took this as a shattering rebuff and assumed the position that if he could not have all of her, he wanted nothing. When asked to characterize her he said, "She was an extraordinarily well-developed girl for her age." The most impressive thing about her, in his opinion, was the generous proportions of her breasts. Since that time he has "constantly thought of her." Detailed examination of these latter thoughts are revealing.

He is obsessively preoccupied with the subject of her breasts. For all these years he has fantasied touching, fondling, and especially sucking them. Their image filled his mind's eye when he masturbated. Presumably, the increase in symptoms is related to his recent divorce. His former wife, a widow, brought two children into the marriage. She is a woman who, according to him, exhibits a domineering attitude he claims not to have observed during their three months of courtship. He regrets the divorce has meant the loss of his relationship with the children whom he "loves dearly." Curiously he expresses

201

no feelings reflecting the loss of love and companionship of his ex-wife! She divorced him because "we couldn't get along together." She, it seems, always wanted to be "on the go" while he, on the contrary, wished to settle down quietly in the midst of his acquired family.

It is quite clear that his attachment at the age of 16 was characterized by an immature quality that fed on itself and required exclusivity but not reciprocity of relationship with the object. That his attachment was primarily an oral one is singularly evident. The sole significant memories of this girl are related to her large breasts. His tearfulness is not at the loss of a person whom he loved, but at the loss of the breast! The girl herself seems to represent no more than a vehicle to which the breasts, whose loss he still mourns, are attached. No doubt the sight of this girl's bosom when he was 16 evoked dormant oral wishes which were merely put aside rather than resolved during his *weaning process*. It was their size that excited him; the girl herself as a personality was ignored. In infancy all breasts seem comparatively huge by virtue of the fact that the measure of "size" is one's own body, and that as one grows in physical stature the real world seemingly decreases. Just as the Lilliputians discovered Gulliver to be a huge giant (an estimate, of course, due to their comparative small size), so it is that the patient "recalls" the breast as huge, whereas to the mother who presented it during his infancy it may have been of quite ordinary dimensions. Thus the maternal breast is invariably "recalled" as having been huge in size. The primitive oral impulses masquerade in the guise of sexuality not only because of the "protective coloring" which the latter provides, but also because of the connections established in the unconscious relating the one with the other. The oral "anlage" for orgasm has already been established so that historically speaking, a very real association does in fact exist. The patient's demand for an exclusive relationship with this girl reflected his desire to continue what during early infancy appeared to him as an exclusive relationship between himself and his mother. His yearning for the girl is a screen-memory; his intense and persistent fantasy focusing upon her breasts is but a thinly disguised symbolic continuation of nursing. In other words, he ruminates, replaying the material ceaselessly so that he is always in the process of being filled. His ego never successfully completed the *weaning process.*

This case is, in my judgment, especially instructive because the content that serves to fill his emptiness emphasises that his primary interest is "breast," more especially "big breasts." As just jointed out, the emphasis on size is the clue to the fact that under the cloak of concern for their size resides an ancient fascination for the maternal breast. Moreover, his seizures themselves are of considerable significance. The absence of typical seizure discharge patterns in the electroencephalogram even during sleep indicates that we are dealing with no ordinary case of epilepsy. The relative ineffectiveness of anticonvulsant drugs also points in this direction. We now understand the primitiveness of the patient's psychic status. We recognize that he has matured physically while his ego continues in fantasy to indulge in the gratifications of nursing formulated in an idiom so proximate to the original that the primitive oral aim and object are barely disguised.

It seems incredible—indeed, unheard of—to imagine that once one has grown to adulthood he could still be symbolically suckling at the breast! Still, no better explanation suggests itself, no other hypothesis so well explains so many of the clinical features. It will be recalled that during the *weaning process* the act of nursing becomes progressively modified as the developing ego's influence makes itself felt. We learned how the *tremor response* was identified as the "anlage" of the physiological event of orgasm, just as the *merging* response was the "anlage" for the psychological component thereof. In this present case we have an opportunity to consider the consequences of fixation very early in the course of the *weaning process.* The seizure can best be understood within the frame of reference appropriate to an early moment of the *weaning process.* Phenomenologically, it fits extraordinarily well with the idea of being a "replay" of the *quiver response.* Thus, the patients circumstances, considered as a whole, can be seen as a kind of dumb show—a pantomime which contentlessly and unremittingly symbolically repeats the nursing cycle of early infancy.

This patient is psychotic, despite the fact there are none of the gross psychopathological findings which are sometimes held to be the *sine qua non* of a diagnosis of schizophrenia. His schizophrenia manifests itself within the configuration of his real and fantasy life. He is frequently in a state of *mergement* via his seizures, and it is on this psychodynamic feature that the diagnosis depends. This man has achieved a rather tenuous equilibrium. The degree of ego immaturity is so profound that there is insufficient capacity to establish a real object relation so essential for psychotherapeutic progress. The history of fraudulence and other evidence of "dishonesty" likewise points to the existence of a primitive omnipotent position in opposition to reality. Evidence of fixation on the part of the body of another without consideration of the whole person should always remind the clinician that while he may assist in putting together that which has been rent asunder, he cannot aid in the construction of a still-fledgling ego in an adult. Insight-directed psychotherapy seems to be effective only where the ego is sufficiently well organized to resist the libidinal temptations of oral *merging.*

Most prospective psychotherapy patients have well-organized warning systems that automatically keep them from treatment when it would, on balance, be hurtful for them. Therapists who do not accept this, or at least take it into account, are constantly disappointed that those whom they judge to be "good candidates" decide to forego the psychotherapeutic encounter. But even so, it is rather important that the physician recognize that psychotherapeutic skills not only have limited applicability but possess self-selected subjects as an absolute requirement of their exercise. For it so happens that a patient may be "persuaded" to try psychotherapy to his great disadvantage and the doctor's discomfort and on rare occasion even danger.

The work of the analysis of the preverbal psyche can be compared, I think, to efforts of a detective who knows the modus operandi of malefactors and attempts to sift out false clues planted to lead him away from the suspect. By combining speculation, inference, and the judicious use of circumstantial evidence, he is able to prove his case.

I have been encouraged in the employment of the deductive technique for several reasons. In the first place, behavior and reactions previously either ignored or not felt of sufficient significance to merit consideration, have been analyzed according to psychophysiological principles and made understandable. Secondly, a "sexual" interpretation of the data with which I have dealt, though perhaps possible to achieve, leaves too much unexplained to throw light on the psychophysiological origins thereof. Thirdly, when considered as a symbolic "replay" of the infantile *merging* response, varying in extent and direction in different individuals, psychotic reactions appear more understandable and their origins more certain than any other extant theory of psychopathology. As techniques based on psychic economic considerations are developed we can anticipate that the immaturity syndromes, by which name all functional psychoses should be called, may become truly treatable in terms of ego maturation. A great deal more needs to be learned. This volume has, so to speak, barely scratched the surface of the implications of the *weaning process*. And lastly, perhaps in time, sufficient will be learned about the *weaning process* to make maturation of the ego possible for an ever-increasing number of infants.

GLOSSARY OF TERMS

Adult Mode

The psychological status maintained by adults when engaged in eating, there being no shift in the state of consciousness nor any diminution of object relationships.

Hunger Tide

The cyclic psychophysiological variations in hunger sensations that occur in the absence of food and drink.

Infantile Mode

The manner in which infants conduct themselves while eating; the observable psychic alterations specific both as to form and relationship to nursing (see *Merge* and *Raptus.*)

Merge (Merging, Merged, Mergement)

An accompaniment to nursing manifested by roving random eye movements, half closed lids, and a shift of consciousness in which the infant is out of contact and psychic relationship with others.

Quiver Response

Convulsoid movements sometimes occurring at the conclusion of a nursing session during which a tonic phase is followed by a clonic phase.

Raptus

An accompaniment of nursing which in time replaces *merging,* manifested by an open-eyed, fixed, unperceiving gaze "hypnotically" fixed upon an object, often the mother's face. It represents a transitional reaction en route to completion of the *weaning process.*

Weaning Process

The progression through a series of specific psychophysiological responses resulting in the transition from the *infantile mode* to the *adult mode* of eating and behaving.